MW00628378

TEACHING
Eutychus

TEACHING
Eutychus

Engaging Today's Learners with
Passion and Creativity

HOUSTON HEFLIN

Abilene Christian University Press

TEACHING EUTYCHUS
Engaging Today's Learners with Passion and Creativity

ACU PRESS

Copyright 2012 by Houston Heflin

ISBN 978-0-89112-230-2

Printed in the United States of America

ALL RIGHTS RESERVED
No part of this publication may be reproduced, stored in a retrieval system, or transmitted in any form by any means—electronic, mechanical, photocopying, recording or otherwise—without prior written consent.

Scripture taken from the HOLY BIBLE, TODAY'S NEW INTERNATIONAL VERSION. Copyright © 2001, 2005 by Biblica®. Used by permission of Biblica®. All rights reserved worldwide.

Cover design by Greg Golden
Interior text design by Sandy Armstrong
Cover photograph by Lettie Morrow

For information contact:
Abilene Christian University Press
1626 Campus Court
Abilene, Texas 79601

1-877-816-4455 toll free
www.abilenechristianuniversitypress.com

For Matalee, Emery, Haven, and Gable—
My favorite students
My favorite teachers

Acknowledgments

Thank you to Phil McKinney, Andrea Morris, Lisa Bosley, Matt Dabbs, Mary Lee Mattis, Chris Pierson, Tim Woodruff, and Chris Hatchett for your partnership in the gospel, and for loving teachers by equipping them for their roles.

Thank you to George Saltsman, Kyle Dickson, Bill Rankin, Lyndell Lee, and James Langford for insights on technology and education. Thank you also to Mike Wiggins for coaching on design.

Thank you to Barry Packer and Slade Sullivan for your creative generosity that influenced this project.

Special thanks to Meredith Platt for serving as an initial editor of this manuscript.

My gratitude is extended to David Wray for the years you've invested as a teacher, mentor, colleague, co-teacher, and friend.

Finally, thank you to Karen, for your wisdom, passion, creativity, and for the Eutychus imagery. This would have been impossible without you.

Contents

STRATEGIES

SPIRIT

EVALUATION

Introduction

Eutychus was the product of teaching's perfect storm: a comfortable position and a lengthy lesson with nothing more for students to do than sit and listen.

On the last day of Paul's visit to Troas the disciples met together in a third-floor room for a meal as Paul taught throughout the evening. His lesson went on for hours, until midnight. And one of the people listening to Paul that evening was a young man named Eutychus, who unwittingly positioned himself in a window of the room to hear Paul teach. Eutychus drifted further and further into sleep as Paul spoke and eventually was so unaware of himself that he fell out of the window (Acts 20:9).

An alluring temptation of teaching is to expect nothing more than for students to sit and listen. Sometimes we expect even less of our students . . . that they simply sit. But teaching is so much more. Learning is so much more!

Teachers lead the learning experience for students and we communicate expectations through our teaching about how engaged students should be. They will either be passive receivers or active explorers.

It's a little harsh to suppose that Paul's teaching that night was dead, but one of his pupils was. I can't help but wonder if a more engaging approach to the teaching and learning process might have prevented Eutychus' slumber. Could Paul have reorganized his time to accomplish the same educational objectives with more group participation and fewer droopy eyelids?

The purpose of this book is to equip teachers with ideas and resources to create more attentive students and more engaging lessons so that students actually learn. To accomplish this goal the book is divided into sections that correspond to the various components of the teaching and learning process. Taken together they make up what I call the anatomy of teaching.

The Anatomy of Teaching

The anatomy of teaching includes:

The **Self:** teachers who lead and facilitate learning.
The **Students:** learners who engage in learning.
The **Subject:** content experienced while learning.
The **Setting:** locations where learning occurs.
The **Strategies:** methods to help students learn.
The **Spirit:** God's presence in learning.
Evaluation: Assessment of student learning and teaching effectiveness.

These are the variables that teachers manipulate in order to create a positive learning experience for students. They provide a framework through which to view the art of teaching, which I propose is best accomplished with passion and creativity: passion for each of these things and the creativity to arrange them in ways that help students learn.

As you can see, student learning is central to effective teaching. It's one of the most important criteria by which teaching should be evaluated. With this in mind, we may need to revive more than our students in our classes. We may need to revive our teaching to create environments where students can learn.

Reading This Book

If you're most interested in creative teaching tips you might jump to the section on strategies. That section is full of creative ideas and practical tips to implement the next time you teach. Or you might choose to read through the table of contents looking for something to help you with a specific issue about teaching that you're facing. Finally, you could read through this material from beginning to end as you would a typical book. Regardless of your approach, I hope it's a valuable resource for you. My desire is for your students to participate in your teaching by pursuing their own learning. If there's a Eutychus in your class, let's get that person engaged!

Thank You

If you're reading this book you're probably a teacher—one of the people volunteering your time and using your talents to help people learn. Because of that I want to say thank you.

Thank you for setting aside time in your week to prepare your lessons.

Thank you for always showing up, even on the days when you don't feel like it.

Thank you for arriving early to welcome people into your class.

Thank you for sticking around after class with those who need to talk or because a parent has forgotten to pick up their child.

Thank you for your ingenuity as you teach when you don't have all the resources you need.

Thank you for the times you've spent your own money to purchase supplies.

Thank you for teaching when a student in your class is derailing the conversation with his comments.

Thank you for the days when you aren't sure the class you just taught made any difference in the lives of your students, but you trust that God can do something with what you just gave.

Thank you for the days when your lesson went exactly the way you had hoped. You hit a home run in class, and the only people who will ever know are the students.

Thank you because you've read the caution in James 3:1 that says, "Not many of you should presume to be teachers" but you feel compelled and do it anyway.

Thank you because your investment is making a difference in your students' lives, which means it's making a difference in eternity.

May God bless you as you teach!

SELF

Students crave good teaching and want teachers to lead them in meaningful learning. May we be those people, who realize how we teach and how we live our lives impacts what they learn.

1

The Anatomy of Teaching

What is teaching? And how do you know when you see it?

I believe teaching is leadership of the learning process. To be more specific: Teaching is leadership of the interactions between the students, the subject, the setting, the strategies, and the self for the purpose of learning. It's a process aided by the Holy Spirit.

Let's take a look at each of these components briefly.

To begin, who are the *students* you're teaching? It may be helpful to consider their age, gender, ethnicity, preferred language, and faith maturity. Are they married, single, employed, or looking for work? Their life situation comes with them to the teaching and learning experience. Learning doesn't happen in a vacuum, which means their emotions are brought, too: anxiety about the coming week at work, frustrations with children, or joy because of good news. The principle to remember is that every learner is unique and enters our classroom with a host of issues and thoughts that will bump around in their hearts and minds as we teach.

But the students are not the only variable in teaching. Learning happens when our students encounter content of some kind. So what is the *subject* or content that you intend to help the students engage? Is it completely new to them or somewhat familiar? Is the content being taught for immediate practical use or for reference later?

In addition to these considerations we might ask what *settings* should be involved? Where could learners have the best chance of engaging the material, learning from it, and remembering it? What role would environment or context play in learning? Are you bound to your classroom? How might a trip into a new context increase curiosity and interest in the content?

As you consider how students encounter content in specific locations you might ask what *strategies* or methods would facilitate the interaction between students and the subject? What's the best possible way to create experiences that will facilitate learning in this environment?

Finally, how does leadership of the *self* influence learning? What can the teacher do to prepare herself for the task of teaching? How can the teacher's presence be used to encourage learning?

An important component of the teacher's life should be a relationship with God that is evident in teaching. So we invite the *Spirit* to be present in learning—the Holy Spirit who counsels, guides, and teaches.

Because teaching is leadership of the learning process, teachers have the ability to influence learning. But too often teachers abdicate their responsibilities as leaders and thereby fail to promote meaningful learning.

It's my hope that we understand the great influence teachers possess and humbly enter the teaching and learning process with the knowledge that we have been given significant authority to influence students' lives. How we lead the interactions among these various components of education impacts what they will learn.

2

The Teacher's Life

Where does the authority of volunteer teachers come from? Does it come from the position itself, from the one inviting them to teach, or somewhere else?

In Luke 4:32 we're told that Jesus' message had authority. And the first commentary by Matthew after the Sermon on the Mount is that "the crowds were amazed at Jesus' teaching because he taught as one who had authority, and not as their teachers of the law" (Mt. 7:28, 29). Jesus' teaching was different. I want to suggest a few ways our teaching should be unique as well.

Effective Teachers Are Learners First

To begin, effective teachers are learners first. This is true both chronologically and as a priority, because you can't teach unless you've learned something. Good teaching emerges from consistent learning. If this is true then the greatest teacher of all time must have been a great learner. We don't usually think of Jesus this way, but listen to what Jesus says about this:

> "Whatever I say is just what the Father has told me to say" (Jn. 12:50).
> "The Son can do nothing by himself; he can do only what he sees his Father doing" (Jn. 5:19).
> "My teaching is not my own. It comes from him who sent me" (Jn. 7:16).

And the Hebrews writer says, "Although he was a son, he learned obedience from what he suffered" (Heb. 5:8).

Jesus listened to God and repeated the things he heard. Jesus also observed God and imitated what he saw. Everything he did was a direct result of what he had learned from the Father.

Not only was Jesus a learner, he also seemed to have this expectation of others: that those who teach have first learned something. Think about the interaction between Jesus and Nicodemus in John 3. Nicodemus was a Pharisee, a member of the Jewish ruling council. I want to give Nicodemus credit for his desire to learn. He approached Jesus (albeit at night) to engage this great teacher in conversation. But during that conversation Nicodemus got hung up on the concept of rebirth by water and the Spirit. When he continued to ask Jesus for clarification, we hear some strong words from Jesus: "You're Israel's teacher and you don't understand these things?" (Jn. 3:10).

Jesus expected a teacher of the law, a Pharisee, to have some basic learning or knowledge if he was going to claim to be a teacher. I think that's a reasonable expectation: that a teacher would first be a learner who continues to ask questions and seek answers about God, life, and the world. Effective teachers are learners first.

But they do more than study and learn in order to teach. They apply what they've learned to their own lives.

Effective Teachers Do What They Say

Listen to Paul's critique of some of the Jewish Christians living in Rome:

If you are convinced that you are a guide for the blind, a light for those who are in the dark, an instructor of the foolish, a teacher of infants . . . you then, who teach others, do you not teach yourself? You who preach against stealing, do you steal? You who say that people should not commit adultery, do you commit adultery? You who abhor idols, do you rob temples?

You who brag about the law, do you dishonor God by breaking the law? (Rom. 2:19-24)

If you're going to teach, you need to teach yourself first. Do what you're telling others to do or your message lacks power . . . it lacks authority.

Ezra is an excellent illustration of this point. In Ezra 7:10 we read that Ezra "devoted himself to the study and observance of the Law of the Lord, and to teaching its decrees and laws in Israel." Ezra was devoted to studying and learning all he could. He then applied that learning to his own life. Only then was he qualified to teach others.

What we're really talking about is integrity. It's a vital ingredient to effective teaching:

—Integrity between our own learning and our teaching.
—Integrity between our own lifestyle and our teaching.

As Parker Palmer has said, "Good teaching can't be reduced to technique . . . . Good teaching comes from the identity and integrity of the teacher invested in [community] . . ." (Palmer 2009).

When integrity isn't present, the people in our classes will notice, which reminds me of James 3:1. It says "Not many of you should presume to be teachers because you know that we who teach will be judged more strictly." Growing up I understood this verse to mean that God would be stricter on those who teach. While I still believe this is true, I've come to learn that there is another lesson in this verse. The people we teach will judge us more strictly. They will be watching our lives to see if we really mean what we say.

Conclusion

The life of the teacher must be consistent with the teaching of the teacher. This has important implications for those who follow Jesus. Our teacher told us: "Go and make disciples of all nations . . . teaching them to obey everything I have commanded you" (Mt. 28:19, 20). The invitation to discipleship is a call for all of us to be teachers—something we are both inside and outside of the classroom.

3

What Is a Teacher?

As I've thought about how to answer the question posed by the title of this section, there are many images that came to mind based on years of education . . . images that are not ideal. I've been taught that a teacher is an expert. She is a disciplinarian. A teacher is the one with the answers and his is the most important voice in the classroom. But what if we saw teachers as something different?

Some of the traditional concepts of teachers can be summarized in the image of a reservoir. As a reservoir, the teacher's primary role is a lecturer, dictator of knowledge, and dispenser of content like water through a dam for learners to receive. While there are certainly times when a teacher shares content unavailable to students, this is not my preferred image for what happens in teaching. Sometimes this type of teacher is referred to as the "Sage on the Stage" who performs for the audience. In response to this moniker, some have proposed that teachers should be a "Guide on the Side." That's more in line with my philosophy of teaching, but still misses the mark just a bit.

So I'll offer three metaphors that I believe are consistent with my definition of teaching. In "The Anatomy of Teaching" I said that teaching is leadership of the interactions between the self, the students, the subject, the setting, and the strategies for the purpose of learning. I think the following three images work better with this understanding of teaching.

Teacher as Hiking Guide

Teachers are those who have traveled a path and return to walk the path again with learners. On this journey the learners travel with the guide who highlights interesting scenic overlooks and other points of interest. But in this metaphor the teacher as guide is also a learner; always learning the mountain again and always seeing things in a new way as she journeys with different travelers.

The guide may not have ascended every mountain that will be explored together, but the guide does have some wilderness survival skills: the guide knows how to make a trip into content without getting lost. The guide also has knowledge of principles that will help in the discovery process.

I heard a volunteer teacher named Sherry from Virginia once call the teacher a "prepared facilitator" of experiences. This is a person who is equipped for the journey and leads the interaction of students with content like a hiking guide facilitates the interaction between the hikers and the mountain.

Teacher as Orchestra Conductor

Teachers are also like an orchestra conductor, leading the interaction of diverse parts to produce an experience. The teacher is a leader who orchestrates multiple variables, blending them together in ways that instruct. They decide volume, tempo, instruments, and arrangement, to produce a symphony of learning.

Teacher as Culinary Host

Finally, teachers are those who prepare and combine content like ingredients into a delightful presentation for students to experience. This metaphor centers on the chef-teacher who gathers the ingredients, mixes them in unique combinations, and arranges them in preparation for the meal. While consuming the content is enjoyable, some find great pleasure in the preparation (study) required. Those who skip the preparations may find that the end result is an imbalanced meal that does little for the educational nutrition of those consuming it.

But when the preparation and ingredients have been combined effectively, the chef, who has made and consumed this meal before, invites a new group of guests to eat the meal together. Furthermore, the teacher invites students to learn how to cook it and serve it to others. Students then become chefs and hosts.

Summary of Metaphors

In each of these metaphors (the hiking guide, the orchestra director, and the culinary host) the teacher is proficient with the content, a leader of experiences, and one who fully engages with the learners in the process of learning. These are three attributes that seem central to effective teaching.

In each of these metaphors, the students are engaged as active participants rather than passive observers. They're hiking a mountain, playing an instrument, or consuming a meal in community. The willingness and desire to participate actively is an important quality of effective learning.

Conclusion

This is admittedly an incomplete list of the many metaphors for teaching. Other authors have suggested that a teacher is "a creator, a counselor, a storyteller, an actor, a scene designer, an authority, an emancipator, and an evaluator" (Pullias and Young, 1968).

Regardless of the image we adopt as a guiding metaphor for teaching, ultimately, we teach who we are. This will be the subject of the next section.

4

We Teach Who We Are

You may have heard it said that character is who you are when no one's looking. While that's true, I also believe character is who you are when everyone's looking. And if you're a teacher, everyone's looking most of the time. The lessons we teach don't stop at the classroom door. How we engage people up and down the halls of the church building on Sunday, how we drive on Monday morning, and where we place ourselves on Friday night all have an impact on our influence as teachers.

In fact, how we live our lives (what we do), often teaches more than what we say. Because people are watching teachers closely, it's important to remember that who we are as individuals and community members matters. Our character matters. And it will be evident in how we live.

Because our true nature will be revealed in our relationships, it's important to attend to our most important relationships as a priority in our teaching.

As we teach, there must be integrity between what happens in the classroom and what happens at home. Our friends, our spouse, and our children should all perceive that we are the same person at home and in the classroom. Remember that when we fail to practice what we teach our message loses credibility. So let's care for those who are closest to us. Remember also that they are the support system we need to function effectively in ministry to others. It does great harm to be inconsistent in our public and private relationships.

If we teach hoping to inspire Christ-likeness in others this must be evident in our lives. When we make intentional discipleship a personal priority our teaching will be more effective. Instead of espousing doctrinal truths from a vacant life we will be manifesting the Spirit of God among the people we teach.

In the mid-twentieth century A. W. Tozer recognized that teachers' lives disconnected from God were threatening effective Bible teaching. He claimed: "There is today no lack of Bible teachers to set forth correctly the principles of the doctrines of Christ, but too many of these seem satisfied to teach the fundamentals of the faith year after year, strangely unaware that there is in their ministry no manifest Presence, nor anything unusual in their personal lives. They minister constantly to believers who feel within their breasts a longing which their teaching simply does not satisfy" (Tozer, 1948, 8).

Those we teach are coming to our classes and small groups not just wanting to hear words about God. They want to connect with God. We can serve them and meet their deepest needs by being connected to God ourselves—by attending to our spiritual health through practices of discipline and discipleship. When we do this, our students will benefit. Because our teaching is not just with words. We teach who we are.

5

Two Essential Qualities of Teachers

What would you say are the most important qualities in a good teacher?

I think we need to answer this question if we're aspiring to be effective in our roles. As I try to answer this question, I can think of some very important characteristics:

—A good teacher should be able to communicate well so that learners understand content.

—A good teacher should listen to learners and their questions.

—A good teacher should lead the classroom environment and the setting of learning.

These are important, but there's more. Jesus understood a few things about good teaching. So when he offered to be a teacher to anyone who would be his student, he made an appeal to his inner nature. He invited people to him by describing the type of teacher he would be.

"Come to me all you who are weary and burdened, and I will give you rest. Take my yoke upon you and learn from me, for I am gentle and humble in heart, and you will find rest for your souls. For my yoke is easy and my burden is light" (Mt. 11:28-30).

Jesus claimed to be *gentle* and *humble* with his learners; these are two essential qualities for teachers. When gentleness and humility aren't part of the teacher's character, the opposite vices can easily emerge. And few people learn from an arrogant, or abusive, teacher.

Arrogant teachers leave little room for learning. Their ego fills the room, pushing out inquiry and exploration. Arrogance needs an audience while humility offers an invitation. An abusive or harsh teacher is one who belittles students, fails to offer people the respect they deserve, or ignores the reasonable learning preferences of students.

The result of arrogant and abusive teaching is usually that students don't learn, or worse, they become like their teacher. Remember what Jesus said in Matthew 10:24, "A student is not above a teacher . . . . It is enough for the student to be like the teacher."

But Jesus wasn't the only one to highlight the importance of gentleness and humility. In Ephesians 4:2 Paul told the church, "Be completely humble and gentle." And in a letter to Timothy, Paul said that God's people should be "kind to everyone" as though it were a requirement for the very next thing he mentions, being "able to teach" (2 Tim. 2:24).

Finally, Peter also understood the importance of our interactions and our teaching as we engage outsiders. These interactions are characterized by "gentleness and respect" (1 Pet. 3:15) which requires the humility to know the value of someone else.

Gentleness and humility are essential qualities for teachers seeking to create a positive learning environment. They're vital for those who know that much of learner motivation depends on the hidden curriculum of how teachers engage their students.

In 2010 Diana Laufenberg presented a speech entitled "How to Learn?" and claimed the education of the future must include three elements: It must permit experiential learning, empower student voice, and embrace failure on the path to discovery. That type of education will be enabled by teachers with the gentleness and humility to encourage students in exploration.

The challenge for teachers is to model the teaching we have received by imitating the one whose gentleness and humility creates space for learning. May we create that space for our students.

6

What Students Want in a Teacher

Have you ever wondered what the people in your class think about your teaching? Not many of us have been evaluated, but if your students could give you a rating, what would it reveal about you?

At one point not too long ago, there was a popular website called "Rate My Professor" that generated a lot of attention. At this site college students could anonymously give a 1 to 5 rating to their teachers for everyone else to see. This was supposed to help future students determine which teachers to take and which teachers to avoid. But reading some of the comments students left with their ratings almost makes you wonder if it doesn't all come down to personal preferences. What if some students just like some types of teachers more than others? What if there's not really a secret to effective teaching because different students want different things?

Stephen Brookfield would disagree. He is the author of a book called, *The Skillful Teacher*. After years of teaching and reflecting on the interactions of students and teachers he believes he has uncovered what students really want in a teacher (Brookfield, 2006, 56).

He claims students want two things in a teacher:

First, they want someone who is *authentic*. You don't have to be extremely extroverted, loud, or charismatic. Students just want you to be honest, and transparent when appropriate. They want to know that you're a real person with emotions, interests, and a life beyond the walls of the classroom. Taking opportunities to reveal this side of yourself will help your teaching because it helps students connect with you as a person.

The teacher's authenticity or lack of authenticity will be evident in how the teacher lives. "What the teacher is as a person is expressed not only in his special knowledge and skills, but also in his attitudes and thought. The kind of person he is speaks in all his behavior, from simple human relations to major decisions. Whether he is inquiring about a student's tennis score or discussing the causes of war and peace his being, the kind of person he is, reflects itself" (Pullias and Young, 1968, 115).

The second thing students told Brookfield they wanted was an *authority*. While this may sound daunting for volunteer Bible class teachers, it simply means that students expect a teacher to have spent time reading, studying, praying, and reflecting on the content of the lesson in preparation for teaching it. Students want to know that you have engaged this material. You don't have to master it in order to teach it, but you should demonstrate a strong familiarity with it.

It's probably no surprise to you that Jesus modeled these qualities in his teaching. We find him practicing authenticity and authority, and it was noticed. Here is what the Sadducees said about Jesus:

—"Teacher, we know that you're genuine . . . and you teach God's way as it really is" (Mk. 12:14, Common English Bible).
—"Teacher, we know that you are a man of integrity . . . and you teach the way of God in accordance with the truth" (Mk. 12:14, TNIV).

The people Jesus taught could tell he was authentic and genuine. They also noted that he was an authority with knowledge of the Scriptures.

Two other words we might substitute for these two virtues are *character* and *competence*. Concerning character: Students want (and need) to know that you are a real person with relationships, beliefs, convictions, passions, and a life outside of the classroom. But inside the classroom, they want to know that you know what you're talking about. They want to follow a leader teacher who is competent in the content of the class.

Another biblical figure who models these traits is Daniel. While we may not consider him a teacher in the traditional sense, consider his life and influence:

"Daniel had distinguished himself among the administrators and other officials by his exceptional qualities . . . At this the administrators . . . tried to find grounds for charges against Daniel in his conduct of government affairs, but they were unable to do so. They could find no corruption in him, because he was trustworthy, and neither corrupt nor negligent" (Dan. 6:3, 4).

He was neither corrupt in character nor negligent in competence. He was a person of authenticity and had authority because of his competence.

This week, whether you're standing before a class or walking across the street, remember that you're teaching . . . and the most effective teachers seem to have these two qualities about them: authenticity and authority.

7

The Teacher's Presence

When I interviewed for my current faculty position, I was required to teach as a guest presenter in a Bible class at the university. On the day I taught I was joined by the regular teacher of the class and two other faculty members who sat in the back of the room, each with a sheet of paper they wrote on throughout my lesson. I was later shown that sheet of paper—an evaluation form to assess the quality of a prospective faculty member's teaching. There were ten or twelve elements being evaluated, but one of the items was simply, "The teacher's presence in the classroom."

Why might the teacher's presence be so important to effective teaching? And what does the presence of the teacher have to do with student learning?

I recently required a group of students to video themselves while teaching a Bible class. Then they watched the video and wrote a critique of their teaching. Their responses coalesced around several points that helped us identify how the teacher's presence impacts learning.

Move Out from Behind the Podium

First, students said they hid behind the podium too much and should have moved around the room.

This principle reminds me of something a hospital chaplain named Krister White once told my students: "Where you place yourself in a hospital room in relation to the patient communicates what you believe about God."

I'd say that where you place yourself in relation to your students can communicate a lot about who you think you are and what you believe about God. It's possible that by standing in one location we unintentionally communicate that we are the only (or most important) voice in the room. Of course, walking around has its hazards as well. You wouldn't want to assign a small group discussion and then hover over a group and intimidate them into silence. We should also be cautious about repeatedly walking around the back of a room as a shark circles its prey. The teacher's physical presence, especially when students are seated, can be perceived in any number of ways: soothing, intimidating, controlling, restricting, or enabling. So use your presence wisely.

On the last day of a semester of teaching I asked one of my classes what they liked and disliked about the course. One student said, "I'll never forget that day you sat down at the table with us to teach. That was really enjoyable because it was like you were on our level." I had no idea that something so simple would be so meaningful or memorable to students. So I sat down the rest of that class period as well.

Be Aware of Body Movements

The second most frequent response by students watching themselves teach concerned nervous or habitual body movements such as clicking a marker, shifting their feet, or flicking back their hair.

Some people love to manipulate things in their hands when they process information. Since teaching requires intense focus and concentration, it's no surprise that we repeatedly see teachers flipping markers, snapping marker tops, or gesturing excessively with a remote clicker for presentation software. I've been that person many times. It's so easy to forget that as teachers we are on display for everyone to see and sometimes what we're doing is distracting to student learning. One teacher might be sitting on the edge of a table that is squeaking with every movement. Another teacher swivels in a chair to think while she talks. Other teachers fidget with a pen in their hands, or their notes, their hair, a ring,

The Teacher's Presence 35

or even buttons on their shirt. In drawing attention to these things, I'm not advocating a stoic, non-expressive presence, but a more self-aware presence. Sometimes the way to get there is by watching a video of ourselves teach.

Avoid Filler Words

Next, students said they used filler words like "um" excessively in their speaking.

Most of us have verbal crutches and use filler words like "um," "like," and "you know." For some reason we convince ourselves that verbalizing these words is actually better than the silence that would exist if we didn't speak them at all. But these words are not better. In fact, they can become a distraction to students who are subjected to repeated uses of useless words.

Speak Loudly

Finally, students said they did not speak loudly and clearly enough.

Being self-aware as a teacher includes the ability to monitor your speaking volume. Most classes don't have microphones and amplified sound, so you have to make the call on your volume. In general, the more people present, and the farther away they are, the louder you'll need to be. Finding the balance can be tricky because landing on either end of the spectrum has consequences: quiet speech can put people to sleep; yelling may lead students to regard you as being angry.

Because most people err on the side of being too quiet, I suggest that most teachers remember to speak loudly enough so that the person who is farthest away from you can understand you clearly.

Conclusion

To review and frame these as principles to recall:

1. Experiment with moving around the room in ways that assist student learning.

2. Be aware of nervous habits that draw focus away from learning.
3. Limit the use of filler words like "um" and other verbal crutches.
4. Speak loudly and clearly so your students will understand what you are saying.

8

Co-Teaching's Rewards and Challenges

If you're looking for a dependable way to cut your teaching workload in half don't assume it will happen through co-teaching. Co-teaching will usually require just as much work as teaching individually, and it often requires more because the time invested in preparation for class is spent with the co-teacher. While the time investment is similar to teaching alone, the benefits can be well worth the effort.

Types of Co-Teaching

There are several expressions of co-teaching:

1. Two or more teachers taking turns leading an entire class time.
2. Two or more teachers taking turns leading parts of a class time.
3. Two or more teachers actively engaged, leading together during a class time.

There is a significant difference between co-teaching where one person is responsible for all the content on any one day (#1 above) and co-teaching where two or more teachers are working collaboratively during the teaching time to help learners learn (#3 above). In the former example, when one person takes one teaching day and a second person is responsible for another teaching day, you're not forced to work as closely together before or during lessons. It's the third scenario (where you're both teaching together) that presents the greatest opportunity for reward—but it has some challenges associated with it.

When two or more teachers are committed to working collaboratively in the teaching time, those teachers will need to meet before the teaching event to prepare. One way to prepare for the teaching experience is to identify who will be responsible for certain parts of the class time. By creating the teaching outline or notes together you're able to see both the big picture of what you're trying to accomplish and the details of how you'll get there.

It's also important for the co-teachers to spend time together before class to build their own relationship, which will be on display when you step into the classroom. The ways you interact—specifically, with humor or not—will be evident in how you teach.

You also need to discuss whether one person can interrupt another person during their presentation. Are you interruptible by your co-teachers? Can they interject a thought or question if they think it will help the learning of the rest of the class? I believe the more you're willing to have a dialogue between the two teachers in front of the class, the better it is for the students.

Here are some of the challenges of making the effort to work collaboratively with another teacher during a class time.

The Challenges of Co-Teaching

1. Committing to a common vision for the class time. What teaching styles will be used? What learning activities will be used? You may like to do things differently than this other person, but you understand this person represents you before students because you are a team. Reaching consensus on a philosophy of teaching and the approach you'll take during this class will be vital.

2. Outlining the various responsibilities each person will have for the class. Who will take the lead? How much time will each

person take? And how will the division of labor be handled. Working together means understanding how each person contributes something to the class.

3. Depending on someone else to do what one person could do on their own. You must plan earlier and be very thorough. Co-teaching doesn't mean less work. It's different work--the kind requiring meeting together, brainstorming, and creating in mutuality farther in advance than you might do when teaching alone.

4. Collaborating with different teaching styles. One teacher may rely heavily on humor while another is more serious in approach. One may tend to speak without inviting participation from students while the other is more open to interruption. Invariably there will be an experience when you recognize, "That's not the way I would have done it." And that's okay. It's one of the realities and challenges of co-teaching.

But there are also benefits to teaching with others. Here are some of the rewards of co-teaching.

The Rewards of Co-Teaching

1. Preparation is more inspired so you have more interesting classes. If the creativity of multiple minds has produced a good learning experience, the students will be more engaged and your learning goals will be reached because there were more voices in the creation of the class.

2. The presentation is more engaging so there are opportunities for students to learn from multiple teaching styles. As different teachers facilitate the teaching time there will be different personalities and teaching strengths represented. Students respond to these in different ways.

3. Participation is shared so the division of responsibilities allows you to include more creativity. Knowing that someone else will lead part of the class time frees you up to be thinking and engaging in other ways during class besides talking, which may include setting up what is coming next.

Ultimately, every opportunity to share teaching responsibilities with others has made me a better teacher. I see the art of teaching in a new way through my teaching partners and I'm exposed to some of the ways my own teaching can improve. If you haven't tried this approach why not find another teacher and collaborate on a series of lessons. Both you and your students will be the beneficiaries of the experience.

9

Roles for Volunteers

An effective class or small group usually incorporates the members of that group into roles of service or leadership that match the needs of the group. As you do this it's important to enlist participation from multiple people; and they need to be doing things that are significant, not just to fill a role. The following is a list of some of the responsibilities for volunteers in classes and small groups:

Host

The class host is typically someone who takes the lead in welcoming the class together and communicating announcements. This person might be the one who sends out emails reminding the class of important information or the topic for the coming week.

Hospitality

While some enjoy speaking in front of groups, there are others who love people but prefer to engage in smaller venues. Those working with hospitality focus on greeting people who arrive, introducing guests to class members, and providing guests with any materials they might need such as a Bible, pen, handout, etc. Often, this role is also responsible for making intentional efforts to welcome others to class by requesting contact information from guests and communicating with those who have visited before.

Prayer

In many classes the host will also lead the ministry of prayer, while other groups choose to designate another person to fill this role. The person responsible for prayer collects prayer items from the group and communicates those needs to everyone else. They may also participate in leading the group in prayer based on what has been shared.

Fellowship and Ministry

The most successful classes and small groups that help people grow spiritually seem to spend time together outside the classroom or normal meeting time. Someone might be designated to facilitate this interaction. Someone could be in charge of coordinating social events for fellowship, breakfast meetings, or family gatherings for class members. This person could also help coordinate ministry and service events to others when needs arise.

Food and Drinks

Many Bible classes and small groups choose to provide food and drinks during their meeting times as a means of hospitality. While small groups often share a meal in a home, Bible classes may choose to offer fresh fruit, doughnuts, muffins, or other pastries, along with drinks such as hot chocolate, coffee, juice, and water. Sometimes the class host or hospitality team will also be responsible for food and drinks. To solicit more participation from class members you could invite others to take this role.

Teaching

Finally, the teaching role is vital for successful classes and small groups. While the teacher(s) may already be designated, you might ask who could be trained and equipped to replace the current teacher? Is there anyone with the interest, passion, and ability who might be mentored to begin teaching and leading in the future? There are probably people who would like to learn more about serving as a teacher, but they may not know where to begin. Existing teachers serve as an excellent resource for those who are interested in this role.

STUDENTS

The students in our classes and small groups are at the center of what we do. Their learning is of utmost importance and should influence how we teach. The ways we engage students impacts how those students learn.

10

Loving Our Students

The relationships teachers form with students are vital to the learning process. The following is a list of principles to remember as we engage those in our classes and small groups.

Use Students' Names

There's no substitute for knowing students names and using them when appropriate. We cross a threshold of intimacy when we use someone's name in conversation. Instead of leaning on a generic greeting, when we speak the one word that's most important to that person, their name, it's like a signal that the relationship is more than a casual or insignificant acquaintance. Using a name gives the relationship more permanence and meaning.

Challenge Your Assumptions

One definition of critical thinking is the ability to challenge ideas we consider to be true. We may be entering a teaching experience with assumptions about our students, but to really know them we have to suspend judgment long enough to listen and learn.

Look at Where They've Been

We all bring the past, including our memories, with us to class. Some people may be coming off of an all-night shift at a hospital. Others are sleep-deprived parents of a newborn. Some may be immigrants trying to learn English; others may have been rejected by another church across

town. Each of these prior events will influence learning when you begin
to teach them. Knowing where they've been geographically, culturally,
and emotionally can help you serve them more effectively. One way to
know where they've been is outlined in the next principle.

Listen to Their Stories

Don't make the mistake of always monopolizing the auditory space
in your class. Let other people talk and contribute by sharing their
thoughts. This has the potential to help them learn as they express their
ideas, it can bless other students, and it might just bless you as well when
ideas are shared that you have yet to encounter.

Use Stories They Connect with

Jesus did this well. As the creator of the universe, he could have told parables about microbiology, electromagnetism, or aerodynamics. Instead,
speaking to people in first-century Israel, he talked about fish in nets,
seeds in soil, and fruit on trees. He spoke the language of the people he
wanted to teach. We have an opportunity to do this as well—to use illustrations and stories from the professional worlds of the people we teach.
We could use illustrations from medicine, electronics, law, or education.
Doing this can help the stories and content come alive with relevance for
the people we're teaching.

Remember What They Don't Know

You may have spent hours with the material you're teaching, but they
haven't. A common truth may be a new insight to someone who hasn't
studied the subject like you have. A skillful teacher will reconnect with
their own enthusiasm and joy of discovery as they lead others to experience these things as well.

Encourage Diversity

So many things have the potential to divide us: age, gender, ethnicity, social circles, income, profession, and the list goes on. Instead of allowing these traits to divide us, they can be embraced as welcomed parts of a learning environment that is educationally richer for having multiple perspectives represented.

Engage Students Outside of Class

Build relationships with class members at their job sites, in their homes, or any locations where they spend time. There are two important benefits to this practice: first, it helps us know them better; it also gives the teacher credibility so that when you are in the classroom the students are more likely to listen and be engaged.

Conclusion

The efforts we make to know our students usually leads to loving our students. When this happens our teaching improves . . . and so does their learning.

11

Motivating Learners

Who is responsible for learner motivation? Is it the teacher? The student? Or someone else?

When I've asked students this question, they immediately acknowledge that both the student and the teacher have some responsibility for learner motivation, but many students emphasize the power of the teacher.

It is difficult to force a student to learn who is set against learning, but we can create an environment more conducive to learning; an environment more hospitable to motivation. Effective teachers can inspire some students who might otherwise disengage to desire to learn. In short, teachers can impact motivation.

By motivation I mean the desire to begin and sustain active learning. A motivated student is one who through curiosity or some other force engages in learning. But think about all the forces that could be at work motivating someone to learn: the desire to master content, the desire to be perceived as intelligent, fear of failure, wanting to impress the teacher, a competitive desire to win at the expense of other students, and the list could go on. People engage in learning for many different reasons, but two categories seem to be helpful as we talk about motivation. These categories are intrinsic and extrinsic motivation.

Intrinsic motivation is the desire to voluntarily pursue an activity. The reasons someone might want to voluntarily engage in an activity include innate curiosity, the compulsion to achieve competence, the desire to cooperate with others, or the pursuit of personal goals.

In contrast, *extrinsic motivation* is the desire to endure one activity for the acquisition of something else that is considered valuable. This secondary incentive may include praise, success, or rewards received as a result of the action.

As you may have guessed, it's best if learners feel the nudge of intrinsic motivation. The extrinsic kind can actually serve as a deterrent to true learning. Let me offer an illustration of this point:

My eighth-grade algebra teacher had a practice of assigning everyone to a chair reflecting how well each person did on the latest test. It was very clear to everyone who was in the first chair and who was in the last one. The result of this arranging was two-fold: it humiliated some students who never could grasp the concepts of algebra; for others, their pride got the best of them as they gloated over their coveted positions at the front of the room. If there was any motivation for me that year it was my fear of embarrassment, on the one hand, and my selfish desire for recognition, on the other. Those deep emotions weren't motivating me to learn algebra. I just wanted to do well on tests and get to a better seat.

It is true that friendly competition in the classroom can be a very effective teaching method, but a competitive environment where students battle against others for recognition and awards can harm learner motivation.

So what can teachers do to promote an environment that welcomes intrinsic motivation?

Provide a Meaningful Rationale for Educational Activities

Students need to know why they're engaged in the learning process. What benefit will they reap? How will this help them in the future? Does any of this matter? When students understand the relevance of the content, they're more likely to pay attention in class. Effective teachers help draw the connection between classroom content and life experiences.

Express Genuine Concern for Students

This is done as teachers listen attentively to comments, welcome questions, affirm student perspectives as valid, and acknowledge that students may have reservations about learning. In addition, engaging students outside of class is an important way to build relationships and foster more motivated learning in the classroom setting. As the saying goes, they won't care how much you know until they know how much you care. This is certainly true of teaching.

Reduce Competitive Experiences That Pressure Participants to Win

Those who are successful in such competitions are frequently more motivated to learn, but the majority who do not succeed are more likely to be discouraged and subsequently unmotivated.

Give Students Appropriate Choices

Students appreciate participation in the learning process. This can be done by offering choices to students in areas such as the order of lessons, which small group they will be in, or choices between equivalent learning opportunities during class.

Let Your Passion for the Content Be Evident

The passion of the teacher expressed in enthusiasm for the content is contagious, causing those who witness it to initiate their own learning and engage in classroom settings.

Conclusion

Our students are unquestionably responsible for their part in the learning process, but teachers have great influence as well. In this role we can create environments of intrinsic motivation that invite participation and inquiry, even when students begin uninterested. Most students seem to

believe that an engaging, passionate teacher can motivate a student to
want to learn.

Some of the material in this section is adapted from Houston Heflin, "Theories of
Motivation and Youth Ministry's Adolescent Learners," *Journal of Youth Ministry* 2
(2003): 57-70.

12

Learning Styles Theory

How do you like to learn? Are you convinced it's different from how other people like to learn?

There is significant evidence to suggest that various people learn in different ways. After all, consider how you prefer to receive directions: Do you prefer to have them written down (e.g., "turn left on Main street then right on Maple") or to have them drawn out as a map so you can picture it in your mind? Most of us have a preference for how we receive directions, which may suggest there are different ways people like to learn.

If we embrace the possibility that people learn differently, we might use language to describe some of those differences, like auditory, visual, and kinesthetic learners. In other words, do some people prefer listening (the auditory learners), some people prefer observing (the visual learners) and some people prefer doing (the kinesthetic learners)?

Think about how you memorize information as you prepare material for teaching:

Are you *visual*?
—Do you see things and later recall what was there?

Are you *auditory*?
—Do you listen and remember information?

Are you *kinesthetic*?
—Do you remember what you've done?

Whether or not you subscribe to the learning styles theory, by understanding how you prefer to take in information you will be able to streamline the process of preparation for teaching. You'll be working more efficiently as you learn your notes and prepare to teach.

We see each of these forms of learning (auditory, visual, and kinesthetic) employed in 1 John 1:1-3: "That which was from the beginning, which we have heard, which we have seen with our eyes, which we have looked at and our hands have touched—this we proclaim concerning the Word of life." John testifies that he has heard, seen, and touched the Word of Life (namely, Jesus).

Thinking of other New Testament figures, we might ask, "What type of learner was Thomas?" who did not accept the testimony of his friends about the resurrection but wanted to see with his eyes and touch with his hands the scars of Jesus.

But a conversation about learning styles theory involves more than auditory, visual, and kinesthetic types of learning. In fact, there are those who call these learning modalities. Learning styles theorists have suggested even more ways people prefer to learn. For example, Marlene LeFever outlines four different types of learners (LeFever, 2001, 131):

—*Analytic* learners enjoy learning alone, and are guided by the overarching question, "What do I need to know?"
—*Common Sense* learners seek practical application and ask, "How does this work?"
—*Dynamic* learners are creative visionaries who ask, "What can this become?"
—*Collaborative* learners enjoy social settings where they engage others and ask, "Why do I need to know this?"

Maybe you've noticed that you like to read books alone to learn and you're convinced you're an analytic learner. Or maybe you crave small group discussions to bounce ideas off others and you're a collaborative learner. It's very possible.

But now that we've had a chance to acknowledge what learning styles theorists propose, let's consider the opposing view. An NPR story that aired August 2011 was entitled, "Think You're an Auditory or Visual Learner? Scientists Say It's Unlikely." In this report a cognitive scientist, Daniel Willingham, claimed there may be too much emphasis on students' alleged learning styles and too little consideration of the content being presented. And I think it's an excellent reminder. To illustrate, let me ask you which country I'm describing:

"This country is a popular destination for millions of tourists for its charming atmosphere . . . . It is the largest country in this part of Europe. It is composed of lush plains, rich mountains and beautiful coasts. Because of its high-yielding resources, it is the lead country in the EU for food exports. Its wine is considered one of the best tasting wines internationally . . . and it is the largest wine producer in the world" (goabroad.info).

That information is one way to learn about a country. But compare that auditory description to a map of France.

How do they teach differently? When it comes to geography, learning must include the visual. Geography requires maps. It's not something you learn best simply by auditory descriptions. But to visit that country and taste its food, and to stand at the top of the Eiffel Tower and feel the wind and the tower sway—that's an even deeper form of learning.

Or consider music. It's one thing to be given a sheet of music with no lyrics. We might wonder what it is.

Compare that to experiencing the sound of the music played that is printed on the page. You not only see it but you hear it. Music is different from geography. It can't be learned primarily through visual means. It must be auditory. But there's an even deeper form of learning when it comes to music—the kind that comes from performing it (the tactile/kinesthetic component).

So let me ask this one piercing question: What is the best way to teach the imitation of Jesus? How should we shape and form disciples?

Is it an auditory exercise? Is it visual? Is it kinesthetic? We could also ask, "Is it analytical, dynamic, collaborative, or common sense?"

Let's enlist all the help of multiple learning styles, multiple learning modalities, and any possible resource to help people engage in discipleship both inside and outside the classroom. Let's also remember that some content is best learned certain ways. When you think about creating lessons, learning styles are one variable to consider; but also consider the material you're teaching. Some things are best taught in certain ways, regardless of a learning style.

13

How People Learn

Teachers typically spend the majority of their preparation time focusing on content; namely, what will be taught. This is unquestionably important. We want to teach truth instead of opinion and the material we're engaging should be worth everyone's time. But often there is little attention given to another, equally important variable in teaching: how people learn.

If we as teachers would pause long enough to ask this one question, "How do people learn?" it might transform our teaching and multiply our effectiveness.

The following list includes some of the most important precursors of student learning. When these things are happening students have a better chance of true learning. And while this list is about the ideal conditions for student learning, it's really about how the teacher teaches. So here are five suggestions for how we should teach:

Make It Interesting

If there is any way to connect students' natural interests to the content, then make that connection. Those students who are already interested in the subject seem to have an advantage in their ability to pay attention during class and recall information later.

If there's not an obvious connection to student interest, one responsibility of the teacher is to invite interest: inspire curiosity, demonstrate one's own passion for the subject, show the relevance of the material, and how it can be used in the future.

Make It Relevant

Content that is only theoretical will be much more difficult to teach most students today who want learning that is useful in some way. If students can see the connection to real life application, they may be more willing to invest energy in paying attention during your teaching.

Make It Multi-sensory

When we think about creating classrooms that are more multi-sensory, we should consider both how content is received by students and how it's manipulated by them. First, let's talk about how content is received.

New content should be presented to students in ways that fit the message being shared. Many times, a little more effort to incorporate audio or video would supplement the content. Content can also be discovered by hands-on engagement with others in groups or on trips out of the classroom. We should always be asking, "How can we help students discover this for themselves?" and, "How can we create problems to solve?"

Once students have received content (either through discovery or some other multi-sensory way), their learning can improve if they are given the chance to do something with that content. Are students asked to do anything with what they've learned besides think about it and recall it later? How can they divide it, connect it to something else, judge its worth against other material, or create something new with it? Lessons where students manipulate material (literally and figuratively) are hard to forget. Students need experimentation.

Make It Social

Students learn a lot from teachers, but they also learn from each other as they share stories from life experiences. Most students benefit from the opportunity to bounce ideas off others and refine their thinking on material. Most students are also able to make better decisions with the input from a group. They are also able to make more emotional connections to the material, which is the final point.

Make It Emotional

Highly emotional experiences are deeply memorable. Moments of paralyzing fear, raging anger, and passionate love stick in our minds. Teachers can use this principle of human nature to their advantage. Not by manipulating emotions, but by incorporating emotional experiences in ways that help students learn. This might mean telling a story, allowing learners to try a new experience, incorporating music, or any number of other methods.

14

Connecting the Generations

You may have noticed that many churches structure their class offerings around age groups or life stages. This makes a lot of sense when you want to teach first graders about using kind words or when you want to teach forty-somethings about healthy communication with their teenager. But are there any times when both teens and their forty-something parents should be in the same class?

And what about the first graders? Is there any content or experience that might benefit both groups learning together?

Here are two examples of programs churches have created to help the generations connect in learning contexts:

Mini-Series of Elective Classes

Some people who attend Bible classes have been going to the same class for years. This is a social experience for many people as well as a learning experience. Those who attend a specific class know most of the people in that class or at least have a group of people they enjoy seeing there. And it's a great thing for classes to build community and enjoy being together. But sometimes a byproduct can be an environment so homogenous that the members start to think alike without significant challenges to their assumptions or logic.

One church saw these patterns at work and set out to address them with two objectives:

1. To increase exposure to those of different age ranges.
2. To participate in a class with content that was of personal interest to the attenders.

To accomplish these goals the church set aside a period of time when all middle school, high school, and adult classes would be dissolved over a six-week period. In their place there would be an offering of classes taught by teachers who were passionate and exceptionally knowledgeable about a specific topic. The classes included an introduction to the Bible, a class on the parables of Jesus, a class on church history, a class based on a recently published Christian book, and several others. Because the middle school and high school students were invited to attend this mini-series of classes, the educational benefits ran in all directions. The younger ones sat in a class with those who are older and learned from their wisdom. The older participants experienced class with the passion, enthusiasm, and wisdom of those who were younger. The teachers taught their material, not only in this setting, but also at another time (later in the year, for example) with a different group of people from the same congregation. This six-week experiment became an experiment in intergenerational connections centered around Bible classes.

"Go and Do" Series

The next idea was conceived by the adult education minister and the children's minister of a church, who both noticed an opportunity for more intentional connections between what parents and children were learning. Over the course of a summer, the church combined three adult classes into one. These three classes had a substantial number of parents with children. The curriculum for the adult class followed the topics and scriptures already prepared as content for the children's ministry.

Three adult teachers collaborated to prepare lessons each week and facilitate the overall plan for the class. Each Thursday every class member received an email explaining what the children's ministry and the adult class would be discussing on Sunday. They could read the scripture beforehand and prepare to be engaged during class.

The content of the adult Bible class on Sunday was presented at an adult level with a reminder that the children were covering the same material on their level in their classes.

At the end of class each week, every class participant was sent an email with two important resources to "go and do" what they learned. The first resource was a set of questions that could be discussed on the ride home or in a conversation later in the week. These questions were intended to spark conversations between parents and children who had both studied the same material in Bible classes.

The second resource in the email was a set of three practical ideas for activities that families could do together based on that text. These activities ranged from writing prayers, reading laments, creating a picture, and praying for those who are sick, among other ideas.

What they discovered in this experiment is that people valued the intentional connection between adult and children's curriculum. Furthermore, parents appreciated the resources that helped them initiate conversations with their children after Sunday morning. Finally, the spiritual practices gave families an opportunity to participate in activities together that connected to the lesson for the week.

Conclusion

Whether you choose to incorporate people of various generations into class time together or find ways to equip them for interaction outside of class time, it's vital for churches to facilitate intergenerational relationships. As the authors of a new book on Christian intergenerationality put it, "All ages learning together can be an effective, powerful, life-changing, and blessed element in Christian formation" (Allen and Ross, 2012, 216).

SUBJECT

Whether we teach beginning with a passage from the Bible or a current event that is impacting our faith, the content we select is significant. What we teach impacts what students learn.

15

What to Teach?

I have a friend named Rachel who's been teaching in churches for over fifty years. She claims that after the Gospels, Romans should be studied more than any other New Testament book. What do you think? Is she right?

My friend's declaration draws us into the theme of this section: What curriculum should be used? To begin with, you might consider your ultimate objectives. If your goal is to educate people so that they have a thorough knowledge of the Bible, you might select curriculum differently than someone whose chief objective is to educate people so that they know the doctrines of a particular faith group. So the first step in deciding what curriculum to use is to revisit your objectives for the educational experience.

One of the assignments I give my students is to create a list of the top twenty Bible stories that everyone should know. It takes them much longer than they expect to refine the list because there is so much quality content to choose from and any decision to include a story excludes something else from a spot on the top twenty list.

Coming at the same concept from a different perspective, we might ask, Which passages of Scripture receive the most attention in our churches? Are there certain parts of the Bible that we cite more than others? Conversely, which parts of the Bible are neglected or avoided? This tells us something about the judgments we're making in regard to what's most important.

These types of decisions are made every week in churches around the world: What will we teach, what will we emphasize, and what will we not teach? But regardless of what is emphasized, most would agree that the Bible should be the primary text as a resource for the spiritual formation of Christians.

Having acknowledged that the Bible should be the primary text, we could ask, "What other content or resources might be helpful in training disciples of Jesus?" What other subjects should be addressed? How about conflict resolution, the spiritual disciplines, church history, world religions, and social issues like poverty? What about parenting strategies, service learning, and understanding the worldviews of culture? Is there a place for systematic theology, financial stewardship, marriage relationships, or justice and reconciliation? You might even offer a class that equips people with skills and resources to improve their teaching.

There are plenty of subjects we might address as the church helps people grow in their faith and maturity in Christ. If you're not sure which of these to teach next you could ask, "What am I most passionate about right now? What do I care deeply about? What have I recently studied that might be a blessing to others?"

Another question to consider is, "What does my class or audience need to hear?" This may or may not be something you've recently prepared. Still another question to consider is, "What situation or event requires a response?"

On the night of April 21, 1999 I was serving as a youth minister at a church just outside Denver, Colorado. I honestly don't remember what I planned to talk about that Wednesday night, but the conversation we did have is etched in my memory. The events at Columbine high school had just occurred the day before and several of our students attending that school were intensely affected by the shooting. The curriculum for that night became listening to testimonies, comforting the mourning, processing experiences, and claiming the promises of a peaceful God who is faithful to save despite the violence in our world. The question of what to teach was easily answered by the events of life.

While it's important to plan what we teach, it's also important to know our context and recognize when to go a different direction.

Finally, if you read this chapter hoping to find a creative idea about what to teach, invite your group to make a list of the twenty most important Bible stories everyone should know, then assign different students to give a sixty-second synopsis of each one.

16

Sequence of Learning

What sequence should be used as we cover the material in classes? Does order of content matter?

Several years ago I was teaching a class of junior high and senior high students. My assignment was to address the baptisms of John and Jesus as it relates to the current practice of baptism in Christian churches. Half way through my lesson on baptism I saw a hand go up in the back of the room. With the candor of a child, this junior high student asked, "Why should you be baptized into Jesus? Is he the only way to God?" Building off of that student's courage, others began to speak up and ask about the exclusive claims of Jesus related to salvation. While I intended to discuss baptism that night we shifted to a conversation about the identity of Jesus. Rather than continue with my teaching notes and curriculum plan, I took a detour and decided that for the following six weeks we would study the major world religions and culminate with an extensive six week look at Jesus, who invites others into baptism and discipleship.

You can see that several decisions were made here. First, a decision had to be made concerning the scope of the curriculum. In this case I was willing to discuss the major world religions in a church education program. If our goal is to help people become more mature followers of Jesus, they need to know about the beliefs of disciples from other faiths who they will undoubtedly encounter.

The second major decision was to abandon any effort to persuade youth that they should be baptized before establishing the identity of the one who calls them to this practice. It struck me that I was inviting them to follow someone they didn't know. I chose to lay the groundwork of teachings from world religions and then focus on the teachings of Jesus. This in turn allowed students to feel as if they were making an informed choice about whom to follow.

So what principles here apply to teachers?

First, we all make decisions about what is in and what is out regarding the material we use. For example, you might choose to sacrifice some of the time you would spend teaching biblical content in order to teach "how we got the Bible" as well as "how to read the Bible," including skills of interpretation so that students can read and study the Bible themselves.

Second, some lessons serve as a foundation to others that build on that topic. And a logical sequence is preferred to a haphazard one.

Let's consider how sequence of learning applies to teaching new Christians. We could introduce the book of Acts to a new Christian because Acts is full of people who are new Christians. But it might be better to head to the Gospels and spend time learning more about Jesus and the stories of his life before moving to the ways that life affected the community of Jesus' followers.

Third, sequence is also important because some content is connected to other content. Consider Hebrews. It seems fair enough to dive right in and study it as any other book in the Bible, but to do so fails to acknowledge the heavy dependence in this book on the Levitical priesthood. It might be beneficial to read Leviticus before studying Hebrews, or at least while studying Hebrews, in order to receive the most benefit.

Third, the season of the year can inform sequence of learning. The liturgical calendar, also called the church calendar, is a sequence of content following seasons of the year focusing on events such as Pentecost and the coming of the Holy Spirit, Advent and the coming of Jesus, Holy week, including the Passover Celebration, Good Friday, and Easter Sunday. You may not have followed the liturgical calendar in the past, but it's a fascinating and useful tool to help direct our attention to spiritual seasons of the year. You can read more about these celebrations in the section on Church Calendar as Curriculum.

So why is sequence important? It gives our students the best chance at true learning.

17

Age-Appropriate Content

In the preceding section we talked about sequence as it relates to learning material. Some content should be covered first. If you're going to teach Hebrews you should visit Leviticus first. And Luke is a great pre-cursor to Acts.

In this section we expand that conversation about sequence to ages of students. Some material should come first and some material should be saved for later.

I coach my second grader's basketball team. Despite my coaching efforts, these seven-year-olds don't understand everything about basketball. They're at a developmental level where we focus on the big things like dribbling, passing, and shooting. They can pick up more skills as they get older. We don't expect them all to have perfect shooting form. We don't expect them to set screens, block out, or run a full-court press. We certainly don't expect them to be able to dunk the ball.

The same thing is true of children and many adults when it comes to Christian education and spiritual formation in Bible classes. You don't ask a kindergartner to stand up in the assembly on Sunday and speak on substitutionary atonement and its connection to the eucharist. Instead we might show children a piece of unleavened bread and say, "Jesus told us to eat this and remember him," or say to them, "This is the body of Christ given for you."

There is appropriate language and there is appropriate content for different ages.

I remember picking up my three-year-old from Bible class one day as the teacher instructed my daughter, "Be sure to tell your parents all about the lesson today." My daughter proceeded to show me the black and white picture from a storybook that she had colored. The picture was of Abraham lunging over Isaac with a raised knife in hand. As you can imagine, I was taken aback. In my opinion, the traumatic image of a parent intending to kill a child is hardly appropriate for three-year-olds. While I hope Bible class teachers will instruct my children in the stories of the Bible, I expect them to use some discretion as they do so. Some things are just not appropriate for younger children—like Genesis 38's sexual imagery and prostitution between Judah and Tamar.

We should teach the entire Bible to students before they leave home, but at the right time. Use wisdom about how detailed to be, especially when teaching other people's children.

I haven't heard of a church that studies Song of Solomon with their second graders. There's a reason for that.

Most churches make wise judgments about content and use selective editing when children are involved. Consider the story of Noah's Ark. We usually don't even call it the story of Noah and the Flood, or the story of Global Destruction. We rarely address the violent annihilation of humanity in this story or describe the details of drowning, although these are prominent themes in the plot. This is because we know small children can learn something from this story about God's love and Noah's obedience without the details of destruction. This story is a great reminder that there is content appropriate for different ages. Paul mentioned this in Titus 2.

Titus 2:1-8

Here Paul speaks to four groups about four sets of content: material for older men, and older women, lessons for younger women, and younger men. Apparently there was appropriate content for each group. And we need to be aware of who is in our classes and small groups. Who is listening as we speak?

My family visited a church one December as a teacher was discussing the story of Jesus' birth. As the teacher elaborated on each detail of the story,, he reached the word "virgin" and started stumbling. It was almost as if he started down that road and realized the assembly was full of small children who were listening attentively to the birth story but who were probably uninformed about the details of sex. Thankfully the teacher made a mid-course correction and abbreviated his comments by saying "Mary was not married." You could sense a collective sigh of relief from parents who were almost propelled into the sex education conversation before they were ready.

So the next time you plan to teach a Bible story with content that may be questionable for children, either inform parents ahead of time that a specific story will be discussed, or teach the story with wisdom and discernment without the explicit details and invite parents to delve deeper into the details of the story at home as appropriate.

18

Church Calendar as Curriculum

If you're facing a teaching opportunity but you're not sure what to teach, let me suggest a good place to begin. And that's with the church calendar. Not the one posted on the hallways of the church office, but the broader church calendar that highlights the significant days and seasons of the year as they relate to the Christian faith.

Before I say more about that, I want to acknowledge that holy days are nothing new. In Exodus 23:14-17, God tells the Israelites that they are to appear before him three times a year:

—At the Festival of Unleavened Bread (and Passover)
—At the Feast of Weeks (Pentecost)
—At the Festival of Ingathering (Tabernacles)

Deuteronomy 16:16 repeats this command to assemble before God three times a year to celebrate what God has done.

In Luke 2 we read that, "Every year Jesus' parents went to Jerusalem for the Feast of the Passover. When he was twelve years old, they went up to the Feast, according to the custom." So to commemorate God's activity in history through days of the year is something God's people have been doing for centuries.

The "liturgical year," also known as "church year" or "church calendar," is a sequence of events and special days that are celebrated by believers. There are significant differences in how these days are celebrated among different Christian groups. But generally there are scripture readings, colors, prayers, and biblical stories that are employed in Christian assemblies during each season to help the church remember God's work.

So what are some of the days and seasons that a disciple of Jesus might celebrate and acknowledge?

The church calendar begins with *Advent*, the season beginning four Sundays before Christmas. Advent is a time of anticipation and hopeful expectation. As the followers of God in the Old Testament waited for the Messiah to come, followers of God today wait for the Messiah to return.

Christmas is a very familiar celebration where the focus is on the Savior's birth into the world.

Epiphany occurs on January 6th, which is twelve days after Christmas. This event marks the revelation of Jesus to the world by the wise men who came to honor the King and proclaim him to others.

Ash Wednesday occurs seven weeks before Easter Sunday and marks the beginning of Lent. Lent is a forty-day season to focus on submission, sacrifice, and self-denial prior to Easter.

Holy Week begins the Sunday before Easter and chronicles the events in Jesus' life on the days prior to his crucifixion. Palm Sunday marks the day he entered Jerusalem on a donkey while the citizens shouted Hosanna and laid their palm branches before him. Maundy Thursday or Holy Thursday is devoted to celebrating the Eucharist or Lord's Supper as Jesus did with his disciples before his betrayal. Good Friday is the day of Jesus' trial and crucifixion.

Easter Sunday is a celebration of the resurrection. Jesus is no longer dead. He defeated death and is now alive. Easter is one of those moveable feasts that is not tied to a specific calendar day like Christmas, which is always on December 25th or Epiphany which is on January 6th. Easter is on the first Sunday following the first full moon after the spring equinox.

The final day I'll mention on the church calendar happens seven weeks after Easter and is called *Pentecost*. The name of this celebration comes from the fact that it is on the fiftieth day following Easter. You'll recall this was the Old Testament Feast of Weeks that was being celebrated in Acts 2 as a day called Pentecost, when the Holy Spirit first came on the believers after Jesus ascended into heaven. Because Easter is a moveable feast, this day also moves between dates in May and June each year.

The time after Pentecost and before the next Advent is called *Ordinary Time.* A better term might be "ordinal" or "counted" time. This season is used to focus on the events after Pentecost, namely, the mission of God through the church acting in the world.

If you've never followed the church calendar, this is a great time to begin. If you'd like some resources to help you learn more you might consider the following websites that have additional information:

textweek.com   elca.org   crivoice.org

It's my hope for you and your class or small group that the church calendar will be a consistent reminder of what God has done as you celebrate the works of the Lord.

SETTING

Whether you teach inside a classroom or inside a home, the setting is deeply connected to content. Where we teach and how we use those environments impacts what students learn.

19

Using Classroom Space

As the leader of the classroom environment, the teacher is like a set designer. It's your job to manipulate the setting, including tables, chairs, floors, walls, ceilings, audio/visual equipment, food carts, and any other objects in a way that will facilitate learning. The first thing to ask is, "What do I want to accomplish in this class?" Once you have the answer you can ask, "How can the setting make learning easier? What's a distraction that gets in the way? And what needs to be removed from the room?"

Because there are certain advantages and disadvantages to almost any arrangement, your task is to pick one that best fits your lesson and resources.

Chairs

If you're in a classroom with movable chairs and no tables, there are some useful ways to configure the room. One large circle of chairs might be the best option if your group needs to look at each other during the lesson. Another option would be to create several smaller circles for small groups to engage in dialog during the lesson. Then there's always the option of putting the chairs in rows facing the front of the room.

This can be useful for classes that use presentation software or depend on lecture as a primary teaching strategy. However you set up your room, remember to be intentional about what the arrangement communicates. If you think it doesn't really matter how the chairs are positioned, imagine how your class would respond entering their classroom with the chairs in a large circle facing outward. There might actually be a time for this.

Tables

Some classrooms use tables in their arrangement. This can be useful if you're expecting your learners to write something or if you have food and drinks as part of your class. One thing tables provide, especially round tables, is a ready-made small group if you need to move back and forth between presenting at the front of class and using groups for discussion.

Walls and Ceilings

But there's more to classroom space than the tables and chairs. The walls and ceilings are valuable real estate in the teaching experience. They're like a blank canvas waiting for someone to splash with color. My dentist has learned this lesson. If her patients are going to be staring at the ceiling, why not place an image of a tropical island paradise in their line of sight? It seems the least she could do to make the experience more pleasant.

How could you use posters with images or poster board with quotes to support the content of the day? What would single words scattered over the floor do to inspire curiosity and enhance the lesson? How would participation be encouraged if you had as many puzzle pieces as you had students and placed one piece in each person's chair, inviting them to work together in uniting the pieces? Or you could use names of Bible stories that must be arranged in some order, say chronologically.

The possibilities are limitless: pictures, posters, and other decorations do influence thinking, mood, and learning. In an adult class discussing the identity of Jesus, I printed off fifteen different depictions of Jesus—of various nationalities and at various times in his life. I then taped these images to the walls of the room before the class arrived. During the lesson I invited the class to move around the room and consider each image. After they had a chance to do this, I invited them to stand next to the picture they most connected with: Jesus as shepherd, Jesus as teacher, Jesus as a boy, Jesus cleansing the temple, Jesus on the cross, the resurrected Jesus, etc., and asked them to explain their selection.

In preparation for a series on Romans, a classroom was covered in Romans quotations printed onto poster board. These poster-quotes were scattered across the floor, taped to the walls, and tacked to the ceiling. You might ask, "Why the haphazard arrangement?" To bring attention to them, of course!

A final variation on this thought is to let the learners join in the process. We can invite others to participate in influencing the environment through the creation of art or written messages that in some way assists in a theme for the room. Small children especially enjoy seeing their artwork displayed in their classroom.

So the next time you're setting up your room for class, take a look around and imagine the possibilities.

20

The Senses
of Teaching

What color is teaching? What does it sound like? How does it feel? What fragrance is teaching? And what is its flavor? Have you ever considered the senses of teaching?

I've always thought that the Passover was such a perfect object lesson. If you were God wanting your people to remember what you had done for them, you wouldn't just tell them to remember—you would make it impossible to forget!

As one of God's teaching methods, the Passover is brilliant, really. During this meal participants see, hear, smell, taste, and touch God's deliverance. The noise of a lamb taken into the home—the sense of loss when it's slaughtered, the smell of wine, the texture of unleavened bread, the taste of bitter herbs, the unavoidable sight of blood. It incorporates all of the senses as it teaches. Of course, the same is true of communion. It's a multi-sensory teaching tool that engages us as we engage it. This leads me to wonder how our teaching makes use of the multi-sensory opportunities at our disposal. Let's take a brief tour of the five senses to see how they might inspire more creative teaching.

Taste —Food and Drink

Why not food? Why not donuts, muffins, fruit, or other breakfast items combined with coffee, milk, or juices for morning classes? It seems as if these help create a welcoming environment for everyone as they enter. It sets a more casual tone and may put people at ease, ready to learn.

If the story you're teaching involves some form of food, consider how that food could be included in the lesson. It might take some creativity but it would be memorable. What would it be like to incorporate the foods we read about in biblical stories: dates, figs, honey, pistachios, bread, fish, etc.

Smell—Aroma

Some people believe smell is a strong pneumonic tool, influencing memory. We could use that to our advantage by connecting a fragrance with a truth about God. What if every time you smelled vanilla, you thought about purity? What if cinnamon meant salvation?

Touch—Texture

What do students in your class feel? Not emotionally, but physically? Some of them shake a hand, turn the pages of a Bible, grip a pen, or hold a hot cup of coffee. What if they could touch a coin, a lamp, or some other artifact from biblical history? Were they physically engaged in the class in some way? This could be something as simple as a hug.

And how might the temperature of the room influence learning?

Hearing—Music

In some classes the Bible isn't heard, so create an environment for listening to what God says. That may mean providing background music for readings.

So much of life involves music. It creates mood, helps people relax, and it offers a sense of familiarity to those who hear it. It removes some of the intimidating silence that occurs as people trickle into a classroom before the teacher begins teaching. Some people are uncomfortable sitting in silence. Music creates ambient sound that reduces anxiety. Even the ambient noise from a fan and the movement of air can be a welcomed enhancement to the setting.

But music is also useful during a lesson to illustrate a point or highlight a learning objective as lyrics align with what is being taught.

Sight—Images

How could lamps provide a different look than the overhead lights in most classrooms?

Would candles help the learning environment?

What images or videos could offer support for the lesson?

What about current images of biblical locations?

What do you expect your class to look at during your lesson?

Here are two examples that illustrate what this might look like in a learning context.

Illustration: Priests

Each year I teach a class on the Jewish priesthood as a metaphor for service in missions and ministry. In preparation I lower the lights and provide illumination with candles. I also change the aroma of the room by spraying cinnamon or vanilla room freshener. I then have harp music playing in the background or audio of a choir singing psalms in Hebrew. On a table in the center of the room there is bread that everyone will eventually consume. Finally, scrolling Scriptures are projected onto the walls reminding the class of the duties of priesthood, such as Zechariah's service while the people worshiped outside. These things connect with student senses in a way that supplement the content and make learning more memorable.

Illustration: Coffee Shop

I recently challenged one of my classes to create a classroom experience that incorporated multi-sensory engagement. They chose a coffee shop as a theme and transformed an otherwise dull room into a scene with artistic ambience. They dimmed the lights, played subtle jazz music in the background, and brewed fresh pumpkin spice coffee in a corner. They rearranged the chairs into groups of two to four for conversations. They also printed off readings from great authors of the past and placed them around the room. The final touch was to offer blank paper and pencils for creative expression through art or writing.

These are just two examples of many ways to help learners learn from the environment. So the next time you plan a class, consider the senses of teaching . . . .

Then, as with the Passover, maybe our classes will have a chance to "taste and see that the Lord is good" (Ps. 34:8).

21

How Jesus Used Setting

Jesus taught everywhere he went. In fact, rarely was he inside four walls when he offered instruction. That was the exception rather than the rule. We find him teaching in many places:

Mountainside	Mt. 24:1, 2
Garden	Mt. 26:36
Lake	Mt. 8:26
Home	Mt. 9:10-13
Cross	Mt. 27:46
Tomb	Mt. 38:9, 10
Fields	Mt. 12:1-8
Cities	Mt. 11:1
Roads	Mt. 20:29-34
Beach	Mt. 13:2, 3
Temple	Mt. 21:12-17
Synagogue	Mt. 4:23
Courtroom	Mt. 26:57-68

He not only taught in many different locations, he also taught at many different life events:

Wedding	Jn. 2:1-11
Funeral	Lk. 7:11-17

Collection	Lk. 21:1-4
Storm	Lk. 8:22-25
Trial	Lk. 22:66-71
Sabbath	Lk. 14:1-6
Traveling	Lk. 24:13-27
Passover	Lk. 22:7-38
Sickness	Lk. 17:11-19
Banquet	Lk. 4:29-32

When in the synagogue, Jesus read from the scrolls. When he was on the mountain preaching to the people he used imagery that the people could see: lilies of the field and birds of the air. His illustrations emerged from the context of the conversation and he was always using opportunities from life to teach a lesson.

22

Creative Locations
for Teaching

In the previous section we saw how Jesus matched the content of his teaching with the location of his teaching. The subject and the setting were in alignment in creative ways that helped people learn. Given the model of Jesus' teaching, would it ever be beneficial to step outside the walls of the classroom to engage students in material that is best learned somewhere else?

How might a lesson on justice, grace, or consequences be enhanced by a courtroom?

What would it be like to read the story of the paralytic lowered through the roof while sitting on a rooftop?

When would the sounds and sights of the ocean highlight the power of God in stories like the parting of the Red Sea?

What biblical stories come to mind when you think of a hotel lobby, a cemetery, or a desert?

What follows is a list of some creative locations for teaching. What lessons might you teach on location?

Home
Vehicle
Hospital
Park
Hotel

Rooftop
Mall
Cave
Field
Ocean
Lake / River
Theatre
Mountains
Playground
Desert
Cemetery
Garden / Vineyard
School
Forest
Courthouse
Airport
Fire station
Restaurant
Library

STRATEGIES

Teachers orchestrate the connections between the students, the subject, and the setting through the use of teaching strategies that match the objectives of the lesson. How we connect students to content impacts what those students learn.

23

Starting Class Well

If you knew the airplane you were on would experience an in-flight emergency, would you pay more attention to those preflight safety announcements? What would make you pay attention? If they used humor? If they had a testimony about how it saved someone's life? What if you knew the flight attendant well?

Airlines are faced with the same educational challenge that teachers face every week: How do you educate people who have heard it before? Especially when over-familiarity breeds complacency.

I learned something about this one day in an airplane preparing to take off. The flight attendant was very serious about her responsibilities as she performed the safety briefing instructions. When she was finished she approached the exit row area looking each passenger in the eye. Those of us in this section were asked to look at her and affirm with a verbal response that we would in fact assist in the event of an emergency. This verbal response is something the FAA requires and something I had done many times before. However, what happened next was very unexpected. Leaning down, the flight attendant looked at me and said, "Now if we have to evacuate, I want you to look outside the window first and make sure it's a good idea to go that way. If not, let's get out the other side of the plane."

I've never had someone discuss the possibility of evacuation so openly! It definitely got my attention. And all the attendant did was present the same old information, but she did it in a new, deliberate, and engaging way.

What that flight attendant did was lead me to a place of disequilibrium, a place where I was unsettled, unsure, and very uncomfortable. That made me pay more attention during the entire flight.

Disequilibrium is a powerful motivator for learning. It creates curiosity leading us to find out more about the subject.

As teachers, we can tap into this powerful force by incorporating intentional actions into our teaching at the very beginning of class to set the stage for the learning we hope will happen. This will look very different depending on the objectives for the lesson, but the goal of the initial activity is to create an attention grabbing experience. This could be a song, a video, a guest testimony, a news story, an image, or even a question.

Think about 1 John. How do you reconcile 1 John 2 with 1 John 3? In 1 John 2:1 we read:

"I write this to you so that you will not sin, but if anyone does sin we have one who speaks to the Father in our defense." At the same time 1 John 3:9 says, "No one who is born of God will continue to sin . . . that person can not go on sinning." Which is it? Do Christians sin or not?

What if the first thing you experienced at the beginning of class was a teacher slamming a roll of pennies against a table so they drop haphazardly to the floor?

The teacher who did this immediately had the group's attention. They wanted to know what was going to happen next. The teacher then invited every person to take a penny, look at the year it was made, and write about that year of their life. This could be useful to begin a conversation about how God has worked among us in the past.

Another teacher entered a classroom silently and wrote the word "Observe" on the whiteboard. She then set a plastic sack on top of a table and started taking out ingredients to create a peanut butter and jelly sandwich in front of the class. She cut it in half before taking a few bites then cleaned up the table and exited the room.

This made some of the students uncomfortable as they wondered what they were supposed to be doing during this time. Others whispered to each other guessing what this might mean. When the teacher re-entered the room a few moments later, the groundwork had been laid to have a conversation about the responsibilities of witnesses to observe, remember, and testify. The learners were invited to retell their version of what had happened over the preceding minutes. No two people seemed to agree on exactly every detail about the order of events or how the sandwich was made and consumed. The class talked about the necessity of four Gospels to get different perspectives on the same life of Jesus and began to ask what type of witnesses to that story we have become.

Conclusion

Whatever hook or introduction you use, realize that the first moments of class are full of opportunity. It's in these early moments of your time together that some students will decide whether to engage or check out. But like a flight attendant who is intentional about her responsibilities, we have the opportunity to look our students in the eyes and, with a little help from experiences of disequilibrium, persuade them to buckle their seat belts and hang on because it's going to be a great ride.

24

Preparing for Successful Lessons

Wouldn't it be great if the next time you taught you didn't have to stay up late the night before to prepare? Wouldn't it be great if the next time you taught you weren't scrambling at the last minute to find an illustration? I think it's possible to make that a reality.

When I asked a group of college students who had taught a class in front of their peers what one thing they would have done differently now that the experience was over seventy-five percent of the students said they wished they had prepared more before they taught.

Let's be honest, preparing to teach isn't always glamorous. When I think of great learning experiences I usually think about what happens in the classroom. I rarely think about how long it took for the teacher to prepare outside the classroom. But that's the focus of this section: What kind of preparation does it take to have a great learning experience with students?

I have a few ideas I want to share that will make your preparation time more effective and maybe even more enjoyable.

Pray for Wisdom

Our preparation is no match for God's involvement in the teaching and learning process. When we partner with God we find the flavor, spice, and excitement of true learning is more likely to occur. As Paul would say to the Colossians, "It is God's energy that works so powerfully in us"

(Col. 1:29). So ask for wisdom and trust in the God who "gives generously to all" (Jas. 1:5). Specifically, we could pray for personal integrity, attentiveness to the task, and the heart of a learner as we prepare.

Begin Preparing Immediately

As soon as you learn that you have a teaching assignment, begin gathering information and start working on your class. Sometimes our first thoughts on a subject are the ones that need to be shared with others. Other times our commitment to study will reveal insights that we consider worthwhile. But the first impressions we have of a subject are important to capture. If for no other reason, by sharing them we will connect with those in our classes who may think the same things. Even if our study time has informed us that we were misinformed, the initial perception can be a great place to launch a class. The best way to capture this first impression is to write, take notes, or record in some way the first thoughts you have on a subject as you consider teaching it.

Use Incubation Time

But don't stop with your initial thoughts. Great teaching usually includes incubation time: the opportunity for thoughts to mature and new thoughts to be added to our understanding of the subject. The farther in advance you learn that you're teaching, the more incubation time you get.

You may have noticed that the mind is a powerful processor of information. When you put before it the words, images, sounds, and other content related to your class topic, you'll find the mind can make progress organizing those thoughts even when you're not intentionally working on it.

With time on your side, the problem won't be finding enough material for your class. You'll be faced with the challenge of having too much, then sifting through what information is valid and what is not.

Having said that, I would much rather have too much material so that there are some things I don't cover than be left with extra time that I don't know how to use. If we've done our homework as teachers, we won't be faced with that awkward position of having unused time in class.

For many of us, the incubation time is only as effective as our system of recording our thoughts during that time. For this we need a good filing system.

Keep Good Files

Begin collecting ideas related to the subject in a file labeled for that class. You might prefer a physical file folder or you might store information in a computer file. The trick is to pick a place where you can easily access the file and add new material as you go along. Designate a place where you can deposit news articles, YouTube video segments, quotes, images, stories, and other artifacts. As time passes and ideas come, this file will grow into a rich trove of resources. These will supplement your lesson and often provide the illustrations and visual content to make a good lesson a great one.

Study and Learn

Create as many opportunities as you can to engage the content prior to teaching. Think about the content at different times of the day and in different settings. This gives your mind freedom to work creatively on the lesson. Consider taking a notepad with you to meditate on the lesson for the week and record any insights gleaned that may have escaped you earlier. Read books on the subject and re-read scriptures in preparation. One teacher read Colossians every day for thirty days preceding a teaching opportunity on that book. That kind of commitment lays the groundwork for a great lesson.

Once you've done these things you're ready to identify student learning objectives and create teaching notes for the classroom experience. That's what we'll cover next.

25

Creating Learning Objectives

I remember the day I decided I wanted to teach. I was sitting in a college classroom where the professor had orchestrated a multi-sensory experience for students. With a few simple resources that included a tape player, an overhead projector, a handout, and dimmed lights, the professor was able to generate curiosity and awe in students. We were excited to learn.

But on this day, it wasn't the use of technology or multiple teaching methods that I most remember. Once the lesson was over, the professor turned on the lights and pulled from his bag copies of his teaching notes for that day, complete with learning objectives. It was striking to see how we had just done everything written on the paper, and it was equally as shocking to realize that it worked. He did what he set out to do. Or maybe I should say, we did what he prepared for us to do. On that day I saw teaching as something more wonderful and inspiring than I ever had before. I saw teaching as a powerful force and learning as an exciting opportunity. I wanted in on this magical art.

I would venture to say that the most common mistake teachers make may be failing to identify and name the specific purpose they have in mind for teaching a lesson. We should always identify the goal(s) we have in mind for a lesson. If the teacher is unclear about why the lesson is being taught, you can bet the students will be confused. When this happens the students usually verbalize frustration by asking, "Why do we need to know this?" Teachers should always be prepared to answer that question. If all we have in response is a meager threat that it will be on a test, we are the ones who deserve a failing grade. Effective teachers know why they do what they do and can justify their actions.

It's usually a waste of time to teach aimlessly. We're certain to miss the mark if we fail to identify a target. Or to use a journey metaphor, if we don't know where we're going we'll likely end up lost. Learning objectives keep us from getting lost. They are the desired cognitive, affective, and behavioral outcomes of a learning experience. They are what the students will experience during the course of the learning time. Learning objectives answer the question, "What will be different at the end of this experience?"

Said another way, they are the things we want students to think about, feel, and do as a result of the class. The best way to make this a probability instead of a hopeful wish is to invite students to engage in these thoughts, feelings, and behaviors while in the classroom setting.

Too often teachers fail to expect anything from students except that they listen, and occasionally think. Learning objectives outline what students will do in addition to listening and thinking. What will they express? What will they analyze? What will they evaluate? What will they create?

To put this principle into practice, let me invite you, right now, to think about your next teaching assignment. Consider the content you'll be teaching and the people in your class. What are your learning objectives? To learn the names of the twelve tribes of Israel? To inspire people to give time and resources to God? To train people in a foreign language in preparation for a mission trip? Is it to connect once again with the emotion of conversion?

Try to identify at least one cognitive, one affective, and one behavioral objective for your lesson.

As you're thinking about the objectives for your classes, let me share the objectives I have for this book:

First, I want readers to feel excited and motivated to teach well. This is an affective—heart—objective.

Next, I want readers to remember principles of effective teaching. This is a cognitive—head—objective.

Finally, I want readers to implement practices of creative teaching. This is a behavioral—hand—objective.

You may be wondering if it matters whether cognitive, affective, or behavioral objectives come first in a lesson. There's no single template to follow. Each lesson will dictate how you approach material and involve students. But the best lessons seem to have all three of these: ideas that promote thinking and challenge assumptions, a practical activity that requires some action be taken, and an appeal to the heart or emotional aspect of our lives that often serves as the inspiration for learning.

Business leaders will tell you any idea worth pursuing must be reducible to an elevator speech. In other words, can you summarize in fifteen to twenty seconds the reason you want to teach this specific class?

If you're willing to put the effort into creating learning objectives before teaching, you'll have your answer; you'll have more engaging lessons, and who knows . . . you may just inspire someone in your class to become a teacher!

26

Creating Teaching Notes

When you create teaching notes there are two essential things to remember.

First, remember your learning objectives, because these guide you in what types of teaching methods to employ during the lesson. If you know your objectives you can tell stories, share content, and create activities that help you accomplish your goals.

I was teaching a freshman university class once and we were discussing the importance of both hospitality and empathy in learning communities. One of my objectives was for students to create descriptions of each term and then identify where these things were present in our learning community. Guided by those goals, I created two specific experiences.

First, the class was divided in half and separated into two rooms. One room was given the concept of hospitality and the other was tagged the empathy room. The students in each room were invited to create images with Play-Doh that communicated the theme of their room: either empathy or hospitality. Once these student-sculptors had time to finish their work, we came back together and discussed these terms while displaying our creations. It was an interesting conversation.

Next, the students were given the assignment to find examples of empathy and hospitality on our campus over the following two days.

They were to bring back photos supporting their claim that these were or were not present among us.

Without first identifying empathy and hospitality as terms to be defined by students I would never have thought to have them create images of those concepts. Furthermore, the assignment to go find images of these concepts emerged directly out of my desire for learners to identify where they existed among us.

So once you establish objectives for the lesson, you're well on your way to a great learning experience for your students. You'll also find that creating teaching notes is much easier.

But there's a second important thing to remember when creating teaching notes. You must *remember what it's like to be a learner.* This memory informs how long you spend on any one activity or section of the lesson.

When you think about classes or presentations you've been a part of, it's likely the ones you enjoyed were those that incorporated multiple teaching methods so that there was not a long span of just one style. It's a really gifted speaker who can keep our attention for twenty or thirty minutes at a time. It's a magical storyteller who can capture our imagination long enough to tell a one hour story. Since we live in a world where it seems attention spans are decreasing exponentially, remember to build movement into your classroom experience—and not just physical movement. By movement I mean diversity in teaching methods that create anticipation, increase involvement, and hold learners' attention.

So when you're creating teaching notes, specify the length of time you believe an activity will take beside each item. Identify how long you intend to be doing that aspect of the class. This will help you plan for the amount of time you have and give you a guideline about when it's time to move on while teaching. As an illustration, you might begin with a ten minute lecture, followed by a five minute video illustration, followed by a seven minute reflective writing assignment, and then invite student responses to a question for two minutes, and so on. Having your class organized in this way keeps things moving in the right direction and helps keep your students' engaged in learning.

To review, the two things that effective teachers remember while creating teaching notes are 1) the learning objectives for the educational experience, and 2) what it's like to be a student. These in turn inform how you put together the teaching notes.

So what does this look like practically? Here's one template that you might follow:

Start with a title or theme that communicates the general scope of the class. This could be the name of a specific Bible story, the address of a passage of Scripture, or a more creative title that begins to inspire interest in the subject like "The Story of the Lavish and Wasteful Father in Luke 15" as a title for the parable of the prodigal son.

After stating the title or theme for the class, list the specific learning objectives you've created. Then, plan an introduction that sets the stage for what's next. Use a hook of some kind that draws learners into the subject. This could be an attention grabbing question, a problem to be solved, a story that sets up the theme of the lesson, or a statement of disequilibrium that creates curiosity.

Next, begin outlining specific teaching methods that help accomplish each of your learning objectives, remembering to note the amount of time these will take. Create experiences that help learners think, feel, and do what you've outlined in the objectives.

Then, consider how you might help learners apply their learning outside of the classroom through an activity of application. Examples of application include: discussion questions for further reflection, an assignment to go and do, additional reading on the subject, and so on.

Finally, end the learning time with a decisive conclusion that helps learners remember the experience. This might be a memorable phrase from the lesson, a quote that summarizes the point being made, a video that emphasizes the theme, or any other resource that could be used to wrap up that time of learning.

This template can serve as a guideline as you create teaching notes. You might choose to adapt it to fit your own style, just keep in mind that the purpose of your planning is to create engaging and effective lessons for your learners.

Outline of Teaching Notes

Title
Learning objectives
 Introduction or hook
Teaching methods matching objectives
Application
Conclusion

27

Bloom's Educational Taxonomy

Not too long ago my wife and I met after school in a second grade classroom sitting in chairs that were entirely too small for adults. We were meeting with our child's teacher for the annual teacher-parent conference to discuss our child's progress. As the teacher outlined what they do in second grade, she pulled out a paper entitled "Bloom's Educational Taxonomy" and said their goal is to help students move up this ladder of reflective thinking.

Professional educators from second grade teachers to graduate school faculty understand the value of Bloom's Educational Taxonomy and its role in education. Volunteer teachers can benefit from it too.

The following explanation is a revision to Bloom's Taxonomy suggested by Anderson and Krathwohl (2001). It varies slightly from the original but it is more consistent with what I believe about learning.

Basically, Benjamin Bloom suggests that there are six different levels of learning and a hierarchy to educational tasks.

At the bottom, or most basic level, students are able to REMEMBER. They remember facts, symbols, words, sounds, locations, or any number of details. This stage acknowledges that an initial exposure to content is necessary for students to do tasks such as recognize images, recall information, label items in a list, quote a passage of Scripture, or tell a story that they've heard.

It's also necessary in order to move to the next level of UNDER-STANDING what they remember. Here students can construct meaning from their knowledge. They not only have the ability to identify a symbol or concept but they can also explain its significance. Activities at this level of the taxonomy require students to interpret and summarize information, demonstrating comprehension.

The next level is to APPLY former learning in a new context based on what a student knows and understands. At this level students complete tasks or use procedures to solve problems. They are asked to demonstrate that they can do something with their learning.

So the first three levels of cognition are to Remember, to Understand, and to Apply.

The next level asks students to ANALYZE. This may involve subdividing content into various parts or comparing and contrasting two ideas as students seek similarities and differences between them. At this stage students differentiate between concepts and students can attribute characteristics to concepts in order to relate them to other ideas.

The fifth level is EVALUATION. Based on what has already been learned, students at this level make a judgment about the value of a concept: whether that's a piece of art, a philosopher's theory, or a decision. Learners critique, judge, assess, and measure as they seek to reach a conclusion based on standards.

Finally, the highest demonstration of cognition and learning is to CREATE something new based on former learning. Students here think creatively and synthesize their learning by reorganizing elements into a different pattern or structure. Tasks at this level might include instructions to generate, plan, produce, or formulate something new.

So to review in order, Bloom's Educational Taxonomy suggests that teachers can help students Remember, Understand, Apply, Analyze, Evaluate, and Create.

But too often we teachers enter class focusing on knowledge and comprehension of a subject, which reflect the two lowest levels on the taxonomy. If this is all we do we really haven't expected students to do anything except listen and think. We can't stop there! We should expect more. Every other level after the first two requires students to do something with their learning, which means we can't lecture the entire class and expect students in that class to demonstrate these higher levels of learning. There will need to be projects, assignments, dialogue, and opportunity for students to do something besides sit and listen.

So how could you apply your knowledge and comprehension of Bloom's Taxonomy in your class this week? I want to give you three ideas:

First, *create tasks (assignments) that require higher levels of thinking and learning.* Analyze your existing class material and evaluate whether your methods are helping people move up this taxonomy of learning. If not, create opportunities in class for students to apply, analyze, evaluate, and create.

Second, *assess students' learning based on higher levels of thinking* rather than simply testing for knowledge and comprehension. Now I understand that "test" and "church Bible class" aren't often used in the same sentence, but for those who do find it helpful to evaluate students, remember to give them an opportunity to demonstrate competence in the higher levels of learning: analysis, evaluation, and creation.

Third, *ask questions that reflect these various levels for more productive discussions.* At this point I want to give you some examples of what this might look like. We're going to use the book of Romans as an example.

Remember
Who wrote Romans? Who are the letter's recipients? Quote Romans 12:1,2.

Understand
Why did Paul write this letter? Summarize the message of Romans.

Apply

How does this letter to a Gentile church inform our worship and Christian life today?

Analyze

Compare and contrast Paul's writings in Romans and Galatians, offering explanations for the differences.

Evaluate

Support or refute this claim: After the Gospels, Romans should be studied more than any other New Testament book.

Create

Create a life of discipleship that is guided by this letter's message.

As one more illustration of the "Create" level, invite learners to write a letter to a church, a family, or an individual in another town offering encouragement while reminding them of the gospel.

Conclusion

As a teacher, you can use this taxonomy to create quality questions about almost any biblical content. To try it out and practice creating these questions; you might begin with the subject of "Creation" or "The Crucifixion." These questions will help create a more engaging conversation as you lead discussions with students. Leading discussions will be the subject of the next section.

28

Leading Discussions

What's the difference between classroom conversations or small group discussions that go well and those that don't? It think it has everything to do with the one leading the experience.

Leading discussions, whether it's in a class or in a small group setting, requires certain knowledge and skills that can be learned by those who want to become more effective.

So here are ten tips that you can put into practice immediately when you're leading a classroom discussion or a small group.

Ask Questions That Help Students Learn

When you ask a question, remember that the objective isn't to trick students with an impossible question to answer. It's not to stump the students to show how smart you are. The goal is to help them think and learn by verbalizing thoughts and engaging in conversation so they can discover truths for themselves.

This teaching strategy has been called the Socratic Method, namely asking questions to elicit verbal responses that help students learn. Again, remember the focus is the students' learning, not getting the correct answer. So be patient and work with whatever answers you receive to help students learn.

Ask Open-Ended Questions

Open-ended questions are different than closed questions which can be answered with a simple short answer like yes or no. Good questions require more than a simple answer. They usually create a sense of wonder; they represent several possible answers, or require some reflective thought. In short, they welcome conversation.

There is a principle that's related to this thought: It's often good to ask questions that increase in difficulty as the lesson progresses, moving from lower levels to higher levels of thinking. To create these questions remember Bloom's educational taxonomy that we outlined earlier. That will give you a template to follow as you create questions.

Tell Your Group Who You're Talking to

Sometimes students aren't sure who is supposed to answer, or if you really expect an answer at all. So specify when questions are directed to one student, directed to all students, or intended to be rhetorical and processed silently.

Allow Silence

Allow silence after you ask a question. Most people need time to think and don't like to be put on the spot to answer a question they have thought little about. Remember that you've had days or weeks to think about the things you're discussing. Some learners will have just begun to think the thoughts you had days ago.

It may seem counterintuitive to be in a room full of people who aren't talking or doing any other physical act. The stillness and silence can be uncomfortable, but it can be a healthy reminder that we live in community and seek discernment in community.

Never Ask a Question You're Not Willing to Answer Yourself

You may enjoy grilling your group with perplexing problems, but at some point someone is likely to say, "But what do you think?" If it will help their learning to delay answering that's one thing, but students have a right to ask the teacher the same questions the teacher asks the students. Your answer might be, "I'm really wrestling with this and I don't know." But you should be prepared to address the question in some way.

Learn to Listen, and Listen Well

This will lead to better conversations, helping students think critically and process information; it will model listening for other students, and it may lead to more questions that should be asked. Specifically, listen for what the students are not saying. Also, listen closely to discern their emotional state while speaking. Are they anxious, happy, concerned, confused, or excited? This will help you know how to respond.

Discuss, Don't Argue

It's okay for the class to have an engaging conversation where people disagree with opinions or positions expressed, but don't allow the conversation to take a turn and degenerate into attacks on individuals. Set the tone for the interaction so that everyone feels safe to share their ideas with each other.

Respond Positively

The way you treat the people in your class says a lot about you. It also shows students whether or not you can be trusted. Many students will refrain from commenting aloud if they've seen other students speak up only to be shot down by a critical teacher who accepts nothing less than the right answer (as that teacher defines it).

Discernment is necessary here. There are in fact some comments that could be made in a class that should be addressed as theologically in conflict with the basic tenets of the Christian faith: "There is not a God," "Jesus is not God's son," etc. Those types of comments can't be passed over to get to the point of the lesson. Other comments, however, may not be what you expected to hear, but you wouldn't say they're wrong. They just don't fit well in the conversation. It's here that the skillful teacher can affirm participants for offering their perspectives while inviting others who may or may not agree.

Encourage Participation

One way to encourage participation in a group or class is to have participants write down their thoughts and responses that you then collect and read to the class. Ideas can remain anonymous until the class identifies one they want to discuss further. A variation of this strategy might be giving your group time to write down reactions. Then they could share these thoughts with a neighbor, getting to express their ideas, before you ask them to share them aloud with the rest of the group.

Have Fun

Finally, learning in community is exciting and fun, so enjoy it. Leading discussions can be an invigorating opportunity to help people be engaged and attentive while they learn from the wisdom of others.

29

Leading Small Groups

If you're going to put people into small groups make
sure you know why you're using this teaching strategy. And make sure
your students know why they're in their groups. Be very clear about your
expectations.

This may mean writing out instructions for the group on paper that
is given to them or projected in a place they can refer back to. What are
you asking them to do, specifically? Some students will not be able to
function as a group without directions. They need guidelines to keep
them on track.

In addition to specific instructions, give students an estimated time
for their conversation and build in some accountability about how the
time is spent. You can do this by having them report back to the larger
class or report back to you, the teacher, about what they did. Will there
be some answer they discovered? A consensus they agreed upon? Is there
a project they completed? Was something produced by the group? How
will they know if they accomplished what you have set out for them to do?

You can see that it may be necessary to be very specific. Here's an
example of an effective small group assignment:

1. Every group member should share a childhood memory of
   celebration.
2. Once every group member has shared a childhood memory of
   celebration, create a list of some of the important elements of

a good celebration that will be written on the board when we come back together.

3. You will have ten minutes to complete these two tasks.

This makes it clear that the teacher expects students to take turns sharing their childhood story with the group. This should be followed by a group conversation in which they create a list that they will write on the board. Notice also that there was a length of time for the group work.

In addition to these clearly communicated expectations, you could go a step further by assigning specific roles to group members. Here is a creative division of roles that I first learned about from an educational innovator, James Langford:

1. Leader—Ask the questions and keep the conversation moving in a productive direction. This person should feel some individual ownership for the outcome of the group time.
2. Reporter—Take notes in preparation to report on the group's conversation to the rest of the class. This person might be more extraverted or skillful at summarizing information.
3. Time-keeper—Watch the time and notify the group when only a few minutes remain in order to manage the conversation time. Keep track of group progress as it relates to time.
4. Referee—Ensure everyone in the group is given a chance to speak while encouraging respect for divergent viewpoints. The referee will help those who may not have the courage to speak up to voice their perspectives and be heard by others.

As a teacher who assigns small group time, you have an important role to play as students meet together in groups. By moving around the room you can position yourself to be available in case there are questions about the assignment. In addition there are several things to be watching for outlined below.

a. Observe who talks, who doesn't, and why this might be. Is it personality? Is it simply their preferred conversation style? Could it be that the subject is too personal? Do some people feel shut out of the group? Are people talking over others or interrupting? If you see a group that isn't functioning well you can intervene and draw out those who haven't participated.

b. You should also pay attention to non-verbals and the emotional state of groups: Is anyone recoiling in frustration or anger? Is anyone embarrassed? You might need to join a group conversation that doesn't have a healthy emotional balance to it.

c. Finally, observe who speakers look at when they're talking. Is there someone who has influence in the group that others are seeking for approval? Sometimes we unintentionally focus on one person when we're talking to a group. It seems as though effective groups include everyone in the conversation so that no one person is the sole focus of the group's communication.

The great risk of small groups, especially those focused on discussion, is that the time spent would be full of shared ignorance or "group think." By giving people specific instructions and giving everyone in the group the opportunity to be heard, it's more likely the group time will result in communal wisdom and critical thinking. These are things that make small groups worthwhile.

30

The Least Effective Teaching Method

I have a friend who's been teaching on the college level for over twenty years. As he prepares students for their roles as teachers, he often asks this question: "What is the least effective teaching method?" And it's admittedly a trick question, but a majority of the students will answer that lecturing is the least effective method.

In response my friend gently corrects his students by saying, "Actually, the least effective method is the one you used the last time you taught, and the time before that, and the time before that." I would have to agree. The least effective teaching method is teaching from one method. It just happens that the one option we lean on more than any other is lecture.

So consider keeping a list of creative teaching methods in front of you while preparing to teach. If nothing else, it serves as a reminder to mix things up a bit and try something new.

In fact, go ahead and make a decision right now that the next time you teach you'll experiment, take a risk, and try a new teaching method.

Consider these questions as you imagine the possibilities:

How would music help your lesson?

Is there a place for art?

What visual aids could you incorporate to illustrate a point?

Would students benefit from a time of reflective writing?

Is there a case study or problem-based scenario that relates to your topic?

How could small group discussion help students learn?

As you think about these possibilities you may be wondering which teaching methods to use in a particular lesson. Well, it depends.

. . . It depends on the subject,

. . . It depends on the students,

. . . It depends on the resources at your disposal,

. . . And to be honest, it also depends on how much time you have to prepare.

One of the best ways to decide which teaching method to use is to consider what specific objectives you have for that learning time. What exactly do you want to accomplish with your lesson? Your objectives will guide the possibilities.

31

Teaching Methods of Jesus

When you think about Jesus' teaching style what one word comes to mind? At one point in my life I would have said "lecture," or perhaps "preaching." And within that framework I would have said "parables." But not anymore.

One day I read through the Gospel of Matthew looking for teaching strategies of Jesus, and what I found was astonishing! My understanding of Jesus and my understanding of teaching was transformed. Jesus was doing much more than preaching, and parables are only one of the many teaching methods he used.

Take a look at some of the ways Jesus taught:

Blessing
"Blessed are you Simon . . . for this was not revealed to you by flesh and blood but by my Father in heaven" (Mt. 16:17).
"Blessed are your eyes because they see, and your ears because they hear" (Mt. 13:16).
"When Jesus had placed his hands on them he went on from there" (Mt. 19:15).

Metaphor
"You are the salt of the earth" (Mt. 5:13).
"You are the light of the world" (Mt. 5:14).

Simile

"The kingdom of heaven is like ..." (Mt. 18:23; 20:1).

"Everyone who hears these words and puts them into practice is like a man who builds his house on a rock" (Mt. 7:24).

Analogy

". . . in the same way, let your light shine before people" (Mt. 5:16).

"It is not the healthy who need a doctor, but the sick" (Mt. 9:12).

Comparison

"Foxes have holes and birds have nests, but the Son of Man has no place to lay his head" (Mt. 8:20).

"If you have faith as small as a mustard seed you can say to this mountain . . ." (Mt. 17:20).

Illustration

"If any of you has a sheep and it falls into a pit on the Sabbath, will you not take hold of it and lift it out?" (Mt. 12:11).

"No one sews a patch of unshrunk cloth on an old garment . . ." (Mt. 9:16).

Disequilibrium

"You have heard that it was said . . . but I tell you . . ." (Mt. 5:21, 27, 31, 33, 38, 43).

Prophecy

"The time will come when the groom will be taken from them, then they will fast" (Mt. 9:15).

"As Jonah was three days and three nights in the belly of a huge fish, so the Son of Man will be three days and three nights in the heart of the earth" (Mt. 12:40).

Application

"Therefore, if you are offering your gift at the altar and there remember . . ." (Mt. 5:23).

Invitation to Discipleship

"Come, follow me . . ." (Mt. 4:19).
"Follow me . . ." (Mt. 8:22).
"Come to me . . ." (Mt. 11:28-30).

Assignment

"Go and learn what this means, 'I desire mercy, not sacrifice'" (Mt. 9:13).
"Go back and report to John what you hear and see" (Mt. 11:4, 5).

Challenge Inappropriate Behavior

"Let the little children come to me and do not hinder them" (Mt. 19:14).
"Put your sword back in its place, for all who draw the sword will die by the sword" (Mt. 26:52).

Affirm Faith

"I tell you the truth, I have not found anyone in Israel with such great faith" (Mt. 8:10).
"Woman you have great faith" (Mt. 15:28).

Ask a Question

"Which is easier to say, 'Your sins are forgiven' or 'Get up and walk'?" (Mt. 9:5).
"What is it you want?" (Mt. 20:21).
"Who do people say the Son of Man is?" (Mt. 16:13).

Ask a Question and Answer it Himself

"What did you go out in the desert to see? A reed swayed by the wind? If not, what did you go out to see? A man dressed in fine clothes? What did you go out to see? A prophet? Yes, I tell you, and more than a prophet" (Mt. 11:7-10).

"Who is my mother and who are my brothers? Here are my mother and my brothers" (Mt. 12:48, 49).

Answer Questions

"Peter came to Jesus and asked, 'Lord, how many times should I forgive my brother when he sins against me?'" (Mt. 18:21).

"Teacher, which is the greatest commandment in the Law?" (Mt. 22:36).

"Are you the king of the Jews?" (Mt. 27:11).

Answer Questions with a Question

"The Pharisees and teachers asked, 'Why do your disciples break the tradition of the elders? They don't wash their hands before they eat.' Jesus replied, 'And why do you break the command of God for the sake of your tradition?'" (Mt. 15:2, 3).

"The Pharisees and Herodians asked, 'Is it right to pay taxes to Caesar or not?' Jesus said, 'Why are you trying to trap me? Show me the coin used for paying the tax. Whose portrait is this? And whose inscription?" (Mt. 22:17-21).

"The chief priests and the elders of the people came to Jesus and asked, 'By what authority are you doing these things?' Jesus replied, 'I will also ask you one question. If you answer me I will tell you by what authority I am doing these things. John's baptism: where did it come from? Was it from heaven or of human origin?" (Mt. 21:23-25).

Quote the Old Testament

"It is written, 'People don't live by bread alone . . .'" (Mt. 4:4).
"Have you never read the Scriptures, 'The stone the builders
rejected has become the capstone . . .'" (Mt. 21:42).

Object Lesson

"He called a little child and had him stand among them" (Mt. 18:2).

Posed Problems to Be Solved

"The disciples said, 'Send the crowds away so they can go . . . buy
food.' Jesus replied, 'You give them something to eat'" (Mt. 14:16).

Taught What Students Were Interested in Learning

"His disciples said, 'Explain to us the parable of the weeds in the
field'" (Mt. 13:36).
"Peter said, 'Explain the parable to us'" (Mt. 15:15).

Communicated High Expectations for Students

"You of little faith, why are you so afraid?" (Mt. 8:26).
"You of little faith. Why did you doubt?" (Mt. 14:31).
"Are you still so dull? Don't you see . . .?" (Mt. 15:16,17).
"Do you still not understand?" (Mt. 16:9).

Evaluated Student Learning

"Have you understood all these things?" (Mt. 13:51).

Offered Forgiveness

"Take heart, son. Your sins are forgiven" (Mt. 9:2).

Prayed Publicly

"Our Father in heaven . . ." (Mt. 6:9-13).

"I praise you, Father, Lord of heaven and earth, because you have hidden these things from the wise and learned, and revealed them to little children" (Mt. 11:25, 26).

Silence

"A Canaanite woman . . . came to him crying out, 'Lord, Son of David, have mercy on me. My daughter is suffering from demon-possession.' Jesus did not answer a word" (Mt. 15:22, 23).

Parables

"Jesus told them many things in parables, saying, 'A farmer went out to sow seed . . .'" (Mt. 13:3).

"Listen to another parable: There was a landowner who planted a vineyard . . ." (Mt. 21:33).

"Jesus spoke to them again in parables saying, 'The kingdom of heaven is like a king who prepared a wedding banquet for his son" (Mt. 22:1, 2).

He Knew When to Stop Teaching

"Jesus withdrew from that place" (Mt. 12:15).

"Then he left the crowd and went into the house" (Mt. 13:36).

"When Jesus had finished these parables he moved on from there" (Mt. 13:53).

"Jesus withdrew privately to a solitary place" (Mt. 14:13).

"Jesus went up on a mountainside by himself to pray" (Mt. 14:23).

"Jesus left them and went away" (Mt. 16:4).

Conclusion

It's clear Jesus was weaving creative teaching strategies into his engagement with people. While he did frequently preach to large crowds he also taught small groups and individuals in ways that matched their learning needs and the content being shared.

32

Giving Assignments

One way to connect the learning in your class to the lives of your students is to offer assignments.

These could be assignments that are due within class time as well as assignments that require additional time or thought that are due at the next class meeting. Assignments help communicate our expectation that students will be involved, and more than that, engaged in learning.

Now, before you object to this idea because it sounds too academic, let me remind you that Jesus frequently assigned homework in the form of tasks to complete or problems to solve. Consider the following examples.

In Mark's account of the feeding of the 5,000 the disciples approached Jesus with the recommendation to send the crowd away who had been listening to Jesus all day and who needed to eat. Jesus responded by saying, "You give them something to eat" (Mk. 6:37). Immediately they told him why that couldn't be done and how much that would cost, to which Jesus said, "Well how many loaves of bread do you have? Go and see" (Mk. 6:38). Considering the size of the crowd, this task may have taken some time to accomplish, but they did it.

There's also one of Jesus' favorite prompts for homework: the word "Go."

"Go and learn what this means, I desire mercy, not sacrifice" (Mt. 9:13).

"Go back and report to John what you hear and see" (Mt. 11:4).

"Go sell your possessions and give to the poor . . . then come follow me" (Mt. 19:21).

"Go to the village ahead of you and you will find a donkey and colt. Bring them to me" (Mt. 21:1-3).

"Go and make preparations for us to eat the Passover" (Lk. 22:8).

In fact, we currently live in the time between an assigned task and when Jesus said it is due. The assignment was given in Matthew 28: "Go make disciples of all nations . . . teaching them to obey everything I have commanded you" (Mt. 28:19, 20).

In one sense, our service as teachers is one way to complete the assignment we've been given. We're making disciples and teaching them to obey Jesus' teachings.

And while you teach, it helps to connect in-class conversations with out-of-class experiences. That's why homework is so helpful. Retention is more likely when people visit content more than once during a week. Assignments can help with that.

33

Using Keynote and Power Point

One of the most useful yet poorly used technologies to supplement teaching is presentation software like Power Point and Keynote. These programs are easy to learn and offer additional visual material for a lesson. In a short amount of time you can have text, images, audio, or video files on display in ways that engage your class and help them learn. But too often presentations are thrown together haphazardly, without much consideration for either logic or aesthetics.

What follows are principles I've gleaned from a few resources on this topic.

One of the resources that has been helpful as I think about my own presentations has been a book called *The Non-Designers Design Book: Design and Typographic Principles for the Visual Novice*, by Robin Williams (2004). I learned about this book from the second resource I'll mention, Dr. Bill Rankin, Director of Educational Innovation at Abilene Christian University. And finally, I'll cite my own trial and frequent error while presenting.

Here are some principles to guide our presentations:

Use Bigger Font
Even though you make presentations on your computer screen other people don't view them that way. They're sitting on the back row of a

classroom or auditorium and will remain disengaged if what you've prepared isn't visible or legible. So make it really big.

Use Fewer Words and More Images

If you can say what you need to say with a word, a phrase, or even better, an image, then do it. Too much text in a presentation can be exhausting. If you must have a quote or passage displayed then limit text to a maximum of about six lines per slide. And again, communicate any concept you can with an appropriate image.

Think of Text as an Image

When you must use text in a presentation, remember that your text functions like an image. Its appearance and presentation are important. In *The Non-Designers Design Book*, Williams calls this issue Proximity.

She says, "Items relating to each other should be grouped close together. When several items are in close proximity to each other they become one visual unit rather than several separate units. This helps organize information, reduces clutter, and gives the reader a clear structure" (Williams, 2004, 13).

Font Matters

Since text functions like an image remember to make your font fit the style of the presentation or the theme of the topic you're discussing. Williams' list of "reliable typefaces" includes: Baskerville, Bodoni, Franklin Gothic, Futura, Garamond, Gill Sans, Helvetica, Optima, and Rockwell.

Also, since text functions as an image in presentations, the location of that text is important as well. It should be aligned consistently; it doesn't matter if it's aligned left, right, or centered, just be consistent. And occasionally you might consider changing the angle of the text along with an image for greater impact.

Maintain High Contrast Between Font and Background

The closer the font is to the background color the more difficult it will be to read. So think about using a light background and a dark font, or a dark background and a light font. This will allow your viewers to see what you've prepared. Also, avoid color schemes that clash.

Be Consistent with Your Theme

Establish a theme with the title slide and build on that theme with subsequent slides that match or follow the pattern of the original. In the same way, be consistent with your transitions so people will know what to expect and not be continually distracted by the random movement between slides.

Conclusion

With just a little effort and intentionality our presentations can become more effective and more enjoyable. Rather than serving to distract, they can help people learn.

34

Mobile Devices and Teaching

More and more students are coming to our classes with mobile devices with an increasing number of functions. Learners can text, call, play, draw, listen, and watch . . . while ignoring our teaching. There are many possible reactions to this reality. We can either communicate our disdain for mobile devices, or we can embrace them as tools in the learning process. What would that look like? What follows are some ideas for using technology to your advantage as a teacher so that students are engaged with technology, doing things that help them learn.

Bible

First, have students read the Bible from their devices. Many apps have several different translations. This might be helpful during a reading to hear different language used. Having students follow along with their Bible app also keeps them slightly more engaged.

Note Taking

Students can use mobile devices to take notes during a class. They might be doing this for themselves or you might invite them to share them with others at the end of class to identify what other students noted was important. You could also assign a student to use their notes to present a review of this lesson at the next class gathering.

Text

When the students in my college classes aren't paying attention to my teaching, I can usually find a mobile device under a table with fingers (or thumbs) typing away. They love to text. So why not invite them to text . . . you. It's relatively easy to set up a free text number through apps such as Textfree, or if you're willing you can let students have your cell phone number. Then, invite a response to a question that students text in. On one occasion I asked students to complete the following sentence: "I doubt . . ." and the responses were excellent material for conversation.

In addition to asking students to respond to you through text, you might invite students to initiate a question or line of thinking during your teaching by texting you what's on their minds during your lesson.

In either case, texting the teacher allows class participants to have access to your attention without speaking in front of everyone else. There are students who need this anonymity if they're going to contribute.

Photo

Most mobile devices allow you to take pictures. This feature can be a useful tool for teaching and learning. Imagine assigning students the task of capturing a visual representation of a concept that you're discussing: love, loneliness, joy, affluence, sacrifice, etc. Once students take the picture they can send the image to you via text or email and designate if they are willing for that picture to be shared with others in class. You could create a visual collage with these pictures in presentation software like Keynote or Power Point.

Polling

Polling is another way to use technology in teaching because of its availability and effectiveness, but it takes a little effort to make it happen. Some blogs allow you to add polls to a web site that your class could visit on their mobile device and respond to a question that connects with the theme for the day.

Shared Documents

I recently gave an assignment to a class where they interviewed people of various professions with two short answer questions. We used a Google Document to capture and compare the responses everyone received. The students were able to access the document on their devices, edit it, and view the responses of others. This collaborative "research" project allowed students to be engaged in the learning process. Instead of me telling students the answers, they were able to discover them together on their own.

Email

The final idea for using mobile devices in teaching is simply email. Specifically, there are many times I want to discuss an image or text or other document during a class time. I can email my students a PDF or other resource at the beginning of class that they reference or manipulate.

Conclusion

We can try to compete for the attention of students by always telling them to put devices away, which is admittedly necessary at times, or we can help students use those devices responsibly during class.

35

Audio and Visual Media

It once was much more difficult to incorporate technology into teaching because of limited access and difficult equipment. Now it's relatively easy to add audio or video to a class experience, but many teachers still hesitate to experiment with these opportunities. Here are some ideas for how you might make an existing lesson more multi-sensory.

Audio Media

—Play music before your meeting time to set the mood
—Play a song during teaching to support a concept
—Use instrumental music as background during prayer
—Use instrumental music during a writing assignment
—Play audio from a news story that fits with the lesson
—Use a clip from a podcast that talks about the subject
—Record your own message to play during your lesson

Visual Media

Why don't we have more maps in adult classrooms? People need help with geography and placing stories in a context. We could provide a map of the OT or the NT stories and then show a map with the current political landscape and the current location of those biblical stories.

Before computers and photocopying there were many people who spent a lot of time creating images of biblical stories by painting them. Specifically, during the Renaissance we find many artists creating images, sculptures, and other pieces depicting biblical characters. A great place to find a collection of these is at textweek.com.

Finally, concerning images, I'll mention that projection through Power Point or Keynote also allows you to display an image to supplement your teaching. It could be anything that communicates a theme for the day or just a picture of nature can create a welcoming backdrop to your teaching. Many students prefer for visual images to supplement teaching because it helps them focus on the lesson.

36

One-Minute Paper, Traffic Signal

One-Minute Paper

The one-minute paper is simply a term for any reflective writing at the end of a class or small group time that offers participants an opportunity to reflect on their learning in that experience. As a teacher you might take the last few minutes of class to have students journal or write about some of the following themes:

a. When was I most engaged in this lesson?
b. What idea, thought, or comment was new or most interesting?
c. What was familiar here that I've learned before?
d. What one point from this lesson is most relevant to me and how I live?

Simply giving students the time and opportunity to reflect on these questions in writing can solidify the content of the lesson in their minds and lead them to think about the lessons after that class time.

The final idea I want to share is a lot like the one-minute paper but with a visual twist. It's called traffic signal.

The Traffic Signal

This is something I first heard about from "The Public Speaker Podcast" in an episode on "How to Fill Teaching Time." The traffic signal is simply a metaphor for reflecting on student learning. Toward the end of a class you might ask your students to think about the colors red, yellow, and green:

Red—What do you need to stop doing as a result of this class? Is there anything that your learning demands you confront as unhealthy?

Yellow—What should you watch out for? What new insight gives you pause, or makes you question your assumptions?

Green—What should you begin doing? Based on the learning experience, what are you prompted to change in your life and start doing differently?

37

Think-Pair-Share, Jigsaw Groups

Think-Pair-Share

The purpose of this activity is to provide learners with the opportunity to think deeply about a subject before engaging in a group discussion. After presenting content or asking a question, invite students to think about their answers on their own. Next, students are asked to pair up with someone sitting next to them to discuss their answers together. Finally, after a few minutes of sharing in pairs, the group is called back together to share what was discussed.

One of the benefits to this sequencing is that it creates space for more thoughtful responses instead of spontaneous comments that may or may not be as beneficial to the discussion.

And there are several variations to the ways think-pair-share can be led. For example, instead of inviting everyone back together to share their own thoughts, you might invite people to share only the ideas that their partner expressed in their group. This engages students on another level of learning as they have to remember and express what the other person said.

I heard another variation to think-pair-share recently that adds another step to the process: which is think, write, pair, share. This added layer of reflective writing, before getting into groups, might produce even more thoughtful responses.

Jigsaw Groups

Give four groups different content to discuss and learn to the best of their ability. Imagine your class is on the book of Jonah. You could give each group one chapter from Jonah to read. Because each group has a chance to read material and discuss it among themselves they have an opportunity to learn it well.

After the four groups have had a chance to learn the material in their chapter, invite the people in each group to number off. Let's say there are six people in each group. After they number off you can create six groups of four people (one from each of the first groups). You now have a representative from each of the first four groups gathered in six groups. Each of the four people in the groups takes a turn teaching their chapter to the others.

One simple variation to this idea is to divide your class in half and invite the two groups to read different, but related, material. Coming back together each group could teach the other half of the class and then have a conversation about how the two presentations are related.

The educational principle here is to give people an opportunity to teach content so they learn it better themselves.

38

Reaction Panel, Role Assumption

The following two ideas allow learners to speak from a perspective that they take. Having learners verbalize their thoughts can help create a more engaging environment and a more memorable experience.

Reaction Panel

In a class of about forty, I once introduced a topic from current events that related to a biblical principle and asked if any students felt like they had an opinion on what had just happened in the news. I then invited five of those students to the front of the class where they sat in chairs as a panel of "experts" that I interviewed. I had prepared five to seven questions that I asked the panel and let them function much like a daily talk show would for the rest of the class to observe.

You can flip this idea around by designating some people at the beginning of class to sit in the back and observe through the majority of class without commenting in any way. Towards the end of the class invite them to the front to share their observations on the conversation. Some people call this a listening group. They are given permission at the beginning to observe first and make the final contributions to the class based on their observations.

Role Assumption

Many students are less inclined to act out a skit or drama in front of others but you can still tap into their creative, artistic side through role assumption. Invite individuals or sections of your class to assume the perspective of a character in a story. They should speak from that perspective during the exercise. Invite responses to a question that allows your class to take on the perspective, emotions, and concerns of their role.

    a. Two sons in the story of the Prodigal son—Should there be a party for the younger son?

    b. Mary and Martha in their home with Jesus—Shouldn't we offer Jesus our best hospitality through preparation?

    c. Peter (walking on water) and Andrew (in the boat)—What were you thinking when you did what you did?

39

Art, Post-It Notes, Selecting a Song

Art

Where does art appear in your teaching? Why not bring colors or paints to class and invite your group to create an image that interprets a concept being presented. Now before you adult teachers start skipping ahead because you think art is only for children's teachers, I want to challenge you to reconsider your assumptions. Having adults diagram a biblical scene can really help with comprehension. Coloring images with the same detail as the biblical authors can drive home a point. The biblical authors emphasized the "green" pastures of Psalm 23, the "scarlet" sins of Israel washed "white" as snow in Isaiah, and the "purple" cloth that Lydia sold in Acts. These colors and our mind's vision of their stories are worth recreating on paper.

One of the ways I've enjoyed challenging adult classes with art is by using Play-Doh as a tool of interpretation and expression. After reading Proverbs 8 and the description there of wisdom, I invite learners to create an image of wisdom. Some of their sculptures are fascinating. The same assignment could be done with any number of Scriptures, like reading Colossians 1:15-20 and then challenging your class to create an image reflecting the power of God in these verses.

Post-It Notes

Write Scripture addresses on these small pieces of paper and hand them out before you begin if you're going to ask students to read during class. It gives learners time to find the address in Scripture and read over it before doing it out loud the first time.

Also, you could use post-it-notes by handing them out to your class to write a word or draw an image in response to a lesson or concept. Then students could post that note on a wall to make a class collage of responses.

Selecting a Song

This creative teaching strategy gives a class the opportunity to select a song that captures the emotion and message of a lesson or story. For example, let's say you're studying Acts and come to chapter 12 and the story of Peter's miraculous escape from prison when he returns to Mary's house with the worshipers gathered inside. The possibility of Peter's escape was so beyond their imagination that when he knocked on the door they didn't believe it. Which of our worship songs would have been good to sing when Peter joined the group? What songs help us communicate to an all-powerful God?

Or in Acts 16, when Paul and Silas were praying and singing hymns to God at midnight, which of our songs might they have sung? To answer this question students have to consider the context, getting inside the minds and hearts of the characters. It's an interesting exercise that can help bridge the distance between biblical stories and our experiences today.

40

Case Study, Competition, Quiz

Case Study

Case studies are real or fictional situations that require a decision to be made in response to the information given. They might be read aloud or distributed to a class on a sheet of paper for everyone to read themselves and then discuss. Cases provide a way to enter life situations vicariously in order to seek solutions. This method is useful if you want students to apply principles to new situations, or seek wisdom in community as they prepare for issues they will likely face.

Competition

To reduce anxiety among participants that you want to assess, consider creating a game show or competition between two groups as you review information. Questions could be asked to each group and a record kept of which team received the most correct answers.

Quiz

A more traditional approach to assessing student learning is through a quiz. This isn't something we typically introduce into Bible classes and small groups but it is one effective way to gauge memory and understanding of important information.

41

Teaching Memorization

Memorization is an elusive skill for many people who believe they aren't good at remembering long sections of Scripture. Some people have ceased to memorize sections of the Bible convinced that they aren't good at memorization, or it's harder than it used to be when they were young, or any number of other explanations.

The good news is that there are secrets to easier memorization. The bad news is that even following these suggestions will take some investment of time and effort. In order to memorize a substantial passage of Scripture we must be willing to consistently engage those Scriptures over a period of time. Many of us need to engage content both visually and audibly until those sights and sounds are seared on our minds and hearts. Having said that, the rewards are worth it. The investment we make in memorizing Scripture always pays for the cost of time.

So here are some ways to memorize a section of Scripture:

1. Silently read and meditate on a passage, slowly adding to what you can recall. This simple method of building on what you remember is one way to ensure you remember the beginning of passages but the ending may not be as easy to recall because less time was spent on it. Because of this, some recommend starting at the end or a passage and working backwards

2. Attach a physical location to various parts of the passage. Envision walking through your house while you recite the passage, which informs how you learn the passage. Begin at your front door and memorize a few lines. Move successively through rooms of your house attaching a segment of Scripture to that room. This trick allows you to connect a familiar image (a location in your house) with Scripture that is becoming more familiar.

3. Record the passage as an audio file and replay it consistently for memorization. Some people prefer to record their own voice while others have encouraged a loved one to read Scripture for them because their voice is pleasant to listen to. Either way, once the file is created, commit to listening to it during your commute, while walking with your mobile device, or any time you can let the ambient sound include Scripture.

4. Transcribe the passage you want to remember by writing it down. Many college students have learned that when they write words on paper (or even type them) they are more likely to remember them. So a process for memorization might include the following steps:

   a. Read the text, b. Write the text, c. Speak the text from your writing, and d. Meditate on it.

Whatever strategy we use, repetition will be required. It is the exposure to the content that is most important. But if we can attach it to a personal motivation for memorization, a story, a location, an event, or any emotional experience, we're more likely to recall content.

Several years ago on the first day of December my wife started a tradition of reading Luke 2:1-18 to our children at bed time each night in anticipation of Christmas. These verses retell the birth narrative and contain many of the exciting figures, images, and phrases we think of at Christmastime. Our children clearly enjoyed the story and heard it every night during the month of December. What we began to realize at the end of the first week was that our children were mouthing many of the words as we read along. By the end of the second week they were repeating the story aloud with us as we read. By the end of the month they had the passage memorized and recited it to us instead of us reading it to them.

That convicting experience reminds me that with a little motivation and consistent exposure to content we can probably memorize much more than we think we can.

42

Ending Class on a High Note

How is your class going to end? It's important to have an exit strategy to the class. Think through your ideal ending. You may not use it. The conversation may take a different turn and you may not reach the point where it would fit in the class, but don't rely on chance to end on a strong note. In a symphony, the final note is often the one we remember. So make the final point or final teaching action an intentional one. Here are some ideas for how to end class:

Prayer
Pray for wisdom to put learning into practice. Pray for the initiative to continue learning. Pray for students by name. But be intentional about what you're saying as it relates to the lesson. You might write out this prayer beforehand.

Story
Tell a story that captures the concept from the day and solidifies the lesson in their minds.

Question
Ask a question that prompts the need for further discovery throughout the week. Ask a question about some lingering issue that needs to be answered.

Assignment

Give an assignment or challenge that requires some action be taken until the next class. For example, you could require students to engage other class participants during the week, complete a handout, practice certain exercises, or do independent research on a subject.

Image

Project an image, play a song, provide a metaphor, or display a cartoon that makes the point of the day.

Testimony

Sometimes you can wait until the end of a lesson to reveal why this content has special meaning to you, or how it has touched you personally as you share a personal story or experience about the content.

Advertise

The final minutes of class are a great opportunity to invite them back again. Make promises that you can keep about what will happen the next time you're together. Offer information about what might be interesting about the next lesson, explaining how this class will flow into the next one.

Application

Spell out how this class is immediately applicable; show them what to do with the content (the teaching, training, or information). Jesus did this when he taught and then outlined the implications: "Therefore, if you're offering your gift at the altar and remember that your brother or sister has something against you . . . go be reconciled" (Mt. 5:23, 24).

Summarize

Invite your class to state one concept or theme that sticks with them from the class. You might also have them express their emotion about the class time in one word. You could also have them summarize the lesson in one sentence. Tell your students at the beginning of the class that they should expect this and be prepared for it.

Blessing

The end of class is a perfect time to offer a blessing over participants that imagines a hopeful future for them. You might use the Aaronic blessing of Numbers 6: "The Lord bless you and keep you . . . ." Or you might use one of the blessings used by Paul in many of his writings, "The grace and peace of the Lord Jesus Christ be with you." Or any number of other blessings. For ideas, check out 2 Thessalonians 2:16 or 3:16.

So let me conclude this section by offering a blessing to you as you teach:

May God our Teacher equip you with wisdom as you prepare and passion as you present your next lesson.

SPIRIT

The Spirit of God is a Counselor and Teacher working through us to inspire, motivate, and convict. As we teach, we join God in speaking truth that corrects, rebukes, and trains in righteousness. The Spirit in teaching impacts what students learn.

43

Leading Spiritual Practices

What are spiritual practices and why do we want them in the classroom?

Spiritual practices, also known as spiritual disciplines, habits of discipleship, or soul training exercises, are useful for helping your class or small group remember that faith is not just something we do cognitively; it influences every part of our lives: our emotions, our actions, *and* our thoughts.

If our ultimate objective is to help class participants grow in discipleship and continue their development as imitators of Jesus, it makes sense we would incorporate activities that have helped people throughout centuries grow in relationship with God. Instead of viewing Bible class only as an hour of thinking or studying, it can be claimed as an opportunity to engage in exercises that help us get healthier spiritually.

As James Wilhoit, a professor at Wheaton College, has said along with his colleagues:

"One of the best ways to help students prepare for the future is by incorporating experience into the present, promoting the gradual internalization of spiritual 'postures' that will continue in the future . . . The most effective means of securing future spiritual depth is through engaging purposefully in spiritual formation activities in the midst of present experiences" (Wilhoit et al., 2009, 161).

These spiritual practices during class time will help our students feel more comfortable in spiritual postures that will serve them beyond the classroom.

44

Guided Prayer with Groups

Many teachers begin or end their classes and small groups with prayer. These prayers can serve many important purposes that support learning and unite the community. There are other ways to use prayer as well. The following list is offered as inspiration while we imagine ways prayer can become more prominent in the curriculum of our gatherings.

Lord's Prayer

The first idea is to incorporate the Lord's Prayer into your class time. You could do this by praying as a teacher out loud each week, invite a different class participant to read it out loud each week, or offer a time of silence so everyone can meditate on it themselves.

Psalms as Prayers

Next, adopt the prayers of biblical figures whose words are preserved in Scripture. Many of these prayers are found in the Psalms, although several other prayers exist in other places such as Hannah's prayer in 1 Samuel 2 or the prayerful praise offered in Revelation 4.

But I want to give you a list of possibilities as you think about the Psalms. These might be a good place to begin with your class or small group community:

Psalms of Praise: 8, 63, 138
Psalms of Lament: 13, 43
Psalm of Repentance: 51
Psalms of Trust in God: 84, 90, 130, 139
Psalm of Humility: 131

Written Prayers

Invite class participants to write down their prayers on paper. This could be a prayer of praise, thanksgiving, trust, intercession, or even a lament. Written prayers are particularly effective in class when the prayer needs to be private or when the content is more intimate, as with a lament. When you give people the time and permission to express themselves to God on paper it can be a deeply meaningful and educational experience.

One-Word Written Prayers

This is something that can be done in large classes to provide a sense of community. Give people the opportunity to write on a whiteboard (or even papers posted on the walls) a word or phrase that represents a deep concern or prayer request. In this act the class is making a word picture or collage of concerns for others to see and pray for, even if those concerns are not fully understood by others. This activity can be facilitated with a time of Scripture reading while people move from their chairs to write their words or you might have a song subtly playing in the background.

Prayer of Examen

St. Ignatius of Loyola (1491-1556) emphasized the prayer of examen as an important component to discipleship. This is something that can be done during a class or small group time as training for the days when you're not meeting.

St. Ignatius suggested that at the end of each day, perhaps on the way home from work if you have a commute of any length, or at bedtime, reflect on the experiences, events, and conversations of the day and ask yourself a few questions:

When were you living in Christ-likeness? Conversely, when did you act or speak from selfishness, fear, or anger? Is there anyone you need to apologize to because of how you treated them? What would you have done differently if you had lived this day in the confidence of your identity as a chosen, loved child of God?

As you make these observations, pray for God to help you confess your sins to those you've wronged, and confront any inconsistencies between your actions and your desire to live like Christ.

Reading Books on Prayer

The next idea is reading prayers written by others. I'll mention just four of the many books containing prayers. The first two books were written by Walter Brueggemann. One is called *Prayer for a Privileged People* and the second is called *Awed by Heaven, Rooted to Earth.* Another resource is the book called *Common Prayer* by Shane Claiborne, Jonathan Wilson-Hartgrove, and Enuma Okoro. Finally, *2,000 Years of Prayer* compiled by Michael Counsell contains words and meditations from figures in church history.

These books hold collections of prayers written by the authors themselves, or by saints who have gone before us. They offer a template for prayer and teach insights about how to pray and give words to our thoughts and emotions when we may not know what to speak.

Antiphonal Prayer

The next idea is called antiphonal prayer. To lead others in this experience you'll need a prayer written out on a sheet of paper or projected in some way with various parts for a leader to read and for the rest of the group to read aloud.

Psalm 136 lends itself to this type of reading with it's repetition that could be adapted for this purpose:

"Thank you Lord, for you are good."
"Your love endures forever."

"Thank you because you are the God above all gods."
"Your love endures forever."

"You are the Lord of Lords."
"Your love endures forever."

"You alone do great wonders . . ."
"Your love endures forever."

Another prayer found in Revelation 15 lends itself to two antiphonal parts that can be assigned to various groups to read.

Fixed Hour Prayers

The next idea is to train your class or small group in the practice of consistent prayer throughout the day with fixed hour prayers. Daniel prayed three times a day, even when the issue was decreed that to pray to any god except King Darius would result in time with the lions. Daniel kept praying. So what would it be like to adopt morning, noon, and evening prayers . . . to pray at set periods throughout the day? Would this help us make prayer a habit so that we find ourselves praying without ceasing as we're told to do?

There is an app in the iTunes store called "HabiTimer" that allows you to quickly and easily set alarms in increments of fifteen minutes throughout the day. You could use this to remind you that it's time to pray. For example, you could set it to go off every hour on the hour all day as a reminder to spend a few moments in prayer.

Using the language of training again, you might practice this consistent prayer with your class or small group by setting a timer to go off every ten minutes. At that point, pause in the lesson or group time to pray. In this way you'll model what you hope to inspire others to do on their own outside of your group time.

Also, I'll mention a tool called Echo Prayer Manager that you can find at echoprayer.com. This prayer tool will allow you to record prayer requests, set alarms to remind you to pray for certain things with email or text alerts and offers a journal for tracking responses to prayers.

Breath Prayers

The next idea for incorporating prayer into your class time is to lead your group in breath prayers. Breath prayers are short one-sentence prayers that can be offered to God in such a way that they align with our breathing. The most famous of these is "Jesus Christ, son of God, have mercy on me a sinner" (which is an adaptation of phrases in Mark 10 and Luke 18).

The basic idea is to meditate on one half of the phrase and say it in your mind as you inhale and then focus on the second half of the phrase and meditate on it, as you exhale. Using the prayer we just mentioned we would inhale while silently saying "Jesus Christ, son of God" and then exhale while praying "have mercy on me a sinner." And we would repeat that prayer as long as we can concentrate on its meaning.

One of the beautiful qualities of breath prayers is that you can be praying at any point throughout your day, even while doing something else: driving to work, walking on a lunch break, or sitting in a meeting. You don't need a Bible, a journal, or any other piece of equipment. You just need to be breathing.

To participate in what this might be like, I invite you now to consider the following phrases and adopt them into your breathing:

As a deer pants for water
So my soul longs for you (Ps. 42).

Give us this day
Our daily bread (Mt. 6).

Speak Lord,
Your servant is listening (1 Sam. 3).

> You are my shepherd
> there is nothing else I want (Ps. 23).

There are many more but these will give you an idea of what works well in breath prayers. I have a list of these that I keep in my car to remind me of the opportunity to pray while driving. One of my favorites is:

> Open my eyes,
> To see what you want to teach me (Ps. 119:18).

Why not go ahead and practice one or more breath prayers right now?

45

Guided Reading with Groups

Wouldn't it be great if our students left our classes nudged a little closer to God? My desire is for students to grow spiritually because of the things we do when we're together. To that end I want to propose three spiritual practices that you can implement the next time you teach that are focused on the reading of Scripture.

Responsive Reading

First, responsive reading. This is one creative way for the Scriptures to be read that helps people pay attention. You'll need some way to get the words in front of your people: either in the form of projection onto a screen or you can print out a sheet with the text to be read. In either case, it's important to denote what will be read by the leader (or teacher) and what the rest of the group will collectively read. You could also divide a class into two halves inviting each group to take turns reading aloud.

The Psalms seem especially suited for this type of antiphonal reading by dividing various psalms into segments to be read. You can also use the verse designations to signal when each group will read. For example, using Philippians 4:4-7 we could have two alternating groups read aloud:

Group A reads verse 4, group B reads verse 5, Group A reads verse 6, group B reads verse 7. You can copy this pattern for any number of passages that match the theme of the class.

Lectio Divina

Lectio divina is a Latin term for "divine reading" or "holy reading." The phrase has come to mean a specific type of Bible reading that encourages repetition and reflection. While there are many ways to do *lectio divina*, the format I want you to know can be summarized in the three acts of reading, reflecting, and responding.

Begin by selecting a passage of Scripture. It could be as short as one verse or as long as an entire chapter. As examples, you might consider Philippians 4:8, Matthew 6:1-4, or Exodus 18:13-27.

After selecting a passage of Scripture you would invite one person to read the passage aloud and allow several minutes of silence for everyone to reflect on what was read. Then you would invite responses to the reading by asking questions such as: What was a word that struck you from this passage? What phrase sticks in your mind?

You would then have someone read the passage again, perhaps in a different version of the Bible, followed by several minutes of silence (and maybe a question to inspire some thinking on the passage): What is the emotion of the text? What is the author/speaker reacting against?

After comments are shared the text would be read a third time in a different version followed by a minute of silence and perhaps a concluding prayer.

This reading, reflecting, responding pattern is repeated several times to help individuals and groups gain insight and understanding that doesn't come with a quick, cursory glance at the text, which is too often the way we read the Bible.

Repetition of Reading

Finally, how would your class or small group benefit from hearing the same passage of Scripture at the beginning of every meeting time? Sometimes Scripture works on our hearts, minds, and lives through repetition over time. By selecting a meaningful passage that focuses on the theme for a series of lessons we can emphasize the message of that passage and support greater learning during that series.

46

Guided Writing with Groups

Most of us spend more time typing on a keyboard than we do writing with a pen. Setting aside time to write our thoughts can be an ancient but simple spiritual practice that helps us slow down and think more deeply about a subject. What follows are three spiritual practices that involve writing.

Reflective Writing / Re-Writing

First, we can encourage reflective writing based on life experiences, or even re-writing a story that is read.

When you ask people to engage in reflective writing from their own life experiences you might have them think about God's activity during the past day, answered prayers they've experienced, challenges to their faith, or joys they've experienced. They can chronicle these and comment on how God might be working.

The second variation of this experience, re-writing a story from Scripture, is a unique experience. To lead people through this experience, begin by reading a story with several moving parts. For example,

Jesus walking on water (Mt. 14:22-33).
Jairus' request for Jesus to heal his daughter and the sick woman they encounter on the way (Mk. 5:21-43).
Sunday morning running to the tomb (Jn. 20:1-9).

Road to Emmaus conversation and evening (Lk. 24).

After reading one of these stories you could invite your class to re-tell the story from a perspective other than the one by the gospel writer. Simply giving people the freedom to re-write the story from another perspective gives them license to highlight parts of the story we often miss.

Naming Gifts from God

The next activity is an exercise in gratitude. While playing a song or reading a Scripture, invite your group to write on a board the gifts for which they're thankful. This communal experience will often produce a sense of joy, and certainly thanksgiving, among those who participate and see what others have written.

Journaling

Invite your class to keep a journal during class and other learning times to note new insights or lessons learned. This could also serve as a prayer journal as we note the ways God has been present among us.

Even if your class doesn't participate in bringing a journal as teachers we can give our classes paper to record thoughts as the class progresses, which often encourages participation through better listening and thinking. Paper not only serves as a tool to record notes. Paper can also be used to react to what is heard or experienced. Students can journal, capture questions they have, or formulate new ideas based on the content and discussion.

47

Guided Speaking with Groups

Speech is a powerful gift. Spoken words can motivate millions and literally move mountains. They also work in more subtle ways within the lives of those who are speaking. The following exercises allow your class and small group to speak about what they understand and believe.

Give an Answer Exercise

This idea for incorporating spiritual practices into your classroom is inspired in part by the admonition in 1 Peter 3:15 to "always be prepared to give an answer to anyone who asks you the reason for the hope that you have."

Invite everyone to arrange themselves in pairs or triads. Each group must decide on one person to begin. Then offer the class a word or question that the first group member must speak on extemporaneously for one minute. Suggestions for these prompts include: What is the gospel? Who is Jesus? Why do you have hope? What is love? What does peace mean to you?

After the minute is over allow people to share their reactions to the activity by asking questions such as "Why was this challenging? What made it possible to do? Etc."

Then offer another word or question and allow someone else in each group to speak for one minute on that topic. In this way we are preparing the people in our classes to engage in conversations about the core elements of our faith.

Testimony

Sometimes we may be so excited about a lesson we've prepared that we fail to hear from the people in our classes and small groups who have something exciting to share about how they've perceived God working. It's often helpful to let people share in response to questions such as: Where has God been active in our lives recently? What blessings would you name that tells of God's presence among us? What are you grateful for that you want to acknowledge?

Sharing Scripture

I've found it interesting that the Scriptures we love best are the Scriptures we know best. Typically the people attending classes and small groups have at least one or more passages of the Bible memorized. If not, they can at least speak about the theme of a passage that touches them. Offer time to do this as a way for participants to share part of who they are. This exercise also has the potential to inspire others to search the Scriptures and begin memorizing additional verses as well.

Evaluation

As you look back on a teaching experience, how do you know if you were effective? How do you know if the students learned anything? Evaluation is an important component of education that impacts what students and teachers learn.

48

Reflect and Revise

When you think of your last teaching experience, what's one thing you could have done differently in the classroom to improve what happened?

A very simple way to improve our teaching is to take a few minutes after each teaching experience to reflect and make revisions when necessary. Ask yourself the type of questions that will help you improve future experiences with that material.

It takes a little discipline but immediately after class is over is when your memory and emotions surrounding what just happened are most acute. Record your responses to these questions:

What worked well? and what didn't work well?

When did the students appear uninterested or bored? What caught their attention?

What questions arose from students as they engaged this material?

Did you have enough material in your teaching notes to responsibly address the topic? How far did you get in the content?

What resources did you find yourself needing that you didn't have during the lesson?

As you think about these questions and answer them, keep a record of this in a file where it can be located easily.

If you're able to take the time after each lesson and ask these types of questions, writing down your answers, it will significantly improve your teaching. Your teaching will not only improve when you teach this content again, your teaching will improve with any subject matter, because you will be critiquing yourself as well as the teaching notes you've created.

49

Evaluation of Teaching

Earlier, I defined teaching as leadership of the interactions between all the variables involved in the learning process: the students, the subject, the setting, the strategies, and the self. And it's a process guided by the Holy Spirit. With this definition we can create a template that's useful for measuring how we're doing as teachers. The following questions are offered as a guide for self-evaluation.

1. Did the teacher (self) treat learners with the respect they deserve as those made in the image of God?

Respond with affirmation instead of embarrassing learners.

Maintain eye contact and listen attentively.

Make the student's learning the focus instead of the teacher's teaching.

Call participants by name when appropriate.

Teach with passion.

Teach with the authority that comes from integrity between public and private life.

2. Was the content (subject) of the lesson biblical and appropriate to the context of the learners?

Teach truth instead of just opinion.

Use language, illustrations, and points that are appropriate for learners.

3. Did the teaching methodology (strategy) account for multiple learning styles?

Connect the content of the lesson with relevant application.

Use a variety of teaching methods to maintain interest in learning.

4. Was the environment (setting) used to promote learning?

Establish a culture of learning through guidelines for conduct.

Address threats to the safety of learners and remove distractions to learning.

5. Were learners (students) motivated with something for them to think, feel and do?

Motivate learners through relationships, emotion, humor and logic.

Teach toward application in thinking (head), feeling (heart) and acting (hands).

6. Was God (Spirit) present and glorified in the experience?

Pray for God's presence before and during teaching.

Watch for evidence that God is convicting, teaching, and inspiring learners.

So to review, we can evaluate teaching by asking the simple question, "How did the teacher lead?" How did the teacher lead the self, the students, the subject, the strategies, and the setting? In addition, was the Spirit of God present and active in the process?

I want to offer a specific challenge as you read this section today. It may take some courage. What would it be like to give a sheet of paper with this evaluation outline on it to one or two people during your next class? Invite them to give you feedback on your teaching based on these criteria.

We may realize there are some things we do poorly and we may learn there are things we do very well. But it's importance to evaluate our teaching because how we teach impacts what they will learn.

50

Evaluation of Learning

How do you know what the people in your class or small group have learned?

One of the best ways to find out is to ask them. This method has been around for centuries: Jesus asked the disciples after washing their feet, "Do you understand what I have done for you?" (Jn. 13:12) and Philip asked the Ethiopian official who was reading Isaiah, "Do you understand what you are reading?" (Acts 8:30).

But there is more to learning than understanding. So how might we assess the quality of student learning?

The following evaluation template is intended for students to complete as a tool to reflect on their own learning at the end of an experience.

1. What do I understand more fully or in a new way? (Cognitive)
2. What emotions did this experience evoke in me? (Affective)
3. What specific actions does this experience lead me toward? What am I able to do that I wasn't able to do before? (Behavioral)
4. How would I summarize the lesson or message of this class? (Educational)
5. Why is this content important? Why does it matter? (Value)
6. How were relationships with others (including other students, teachers, and the world) influenced by this experience? (Social)

7. How is my understanding of myself impacted by this experience? (Personal)
8. To what degree did this experience nudge me toward greater Christ-likeness? (Spiritual)
9. How much effort did I exert in this learning experience? (Effort)

51

Offer Feedback to Students

In the book *How Learning Works,* the authors claim "to develop mastery, students must acquire skills and practice integrating them." In addition, "goal-directed practice coupled with targeted feedback enhances the quality of students' learning" (Ambrose, et al, 2010, 6). When I read that for the first time, I immediately realized how little targeted feedback I was offering my students.

Looking to Jesus' life we see that he frequently offered feedback: "You are right in saying . . ."; "You are not far from the kingdom of heaven . . ."; "Blessed are you Simon . . ."; "Get behind me Satan . . . ."

In each of these cases the feedback offered the students an idea of how they were performing relative to the teacher's expectations. I wonder if our students know what we expect from them? And I wonder if feedback makes a difference. I decided to test the value of feedback one day with my students.

The Feedback Hoop

I took a group of thirteen college students to a gym during class time one day for an experiment. There were seven women and six men in the class and not one of them had played organized basketball in their former schooling. After conducting a five-minute teaching time on shooting free-throws and demonstrating the mechanics of shooting in front of them, I invited each of them to attempt a free throw.

Only one out of thirteen made a basket. I then asked them to shoot again. This time, a different person was successful, but again it was only one out of thirteen who made a free throw.

At this point I paused to offer some more instruction based on what I was seeing. I reminded them to believe that they could do this and to envision the ball going through the basket. I reminded them to use their legs to get the ball up over the rim and that if you're going to miss either long or short it's better to miss long because you're more likely to make the basket as the ball bounces off the backboard. I told them to take their time when they get to the line and really concentrate. The final thing I did was to ask each one of them what they were going to do differently on this final attempt. Every person verbalized something: "I'll believe in myself," "I'll use my legs," "I'll follow through on my shot." And they lined up to shoot.

This time five people made a basket. That's a significant improvement.

My class on the basketball court was an experiment that put principles of teaching and feedback to the test. I wanted to know what variables would help my students' performance improve over time?

After they had experience practicing the task and after they were given some basic instruction, there was still room for improvement. It was when I gave them targeted feedback based on their prior actions and invited them to evaluate their own performance that their performance improved.

As teachers, part of our job is to guide, counsel, evaluate performance, and offer feedback to students. Of course, this must be done in the humility that comes from keeping the story of planks and specks in our mind's eye. If we are willing to gently instruct our students on their path of learning we may discover an increase in their performance as disciples of Jesus.

52

Learning from Other Teachers

I once met with a delightful group of volunteer teachers at a church in Fairfax, Virginia. One of the assignments I gave them was to create a list of creative teaching strategies that engage the mind and the body in classes. The ideas they came up with were brilliant. Simply gathering teachers to share ideas provided an opportunity for good ideas to be heard and creative teachers were validated. Of course, as these teachers take what they heard back to their classes, the students become the real beneficiaries of this cross-pollination of ideas.

Gathering teachers for a brainstorming and idea-sharing session is an excellent step in improving our teaching. Another form of learning comes from visiting each others' classes:

"There is only one honest way to evaluate the many varieties of good teaching with the subtlety required: it is called being there. We must observe each other teach, at least occasionally —and we must spend more time talking to each other about teaching" (Palmer, 1997, 143). So beginning with "being there," here are some ideas for how to learn from other teachers:

Watch what works well that others do by visiting their classes.

Ask other teachers about their "best practices" or the things they believe improve the quality of teaching.

Reflect on your own teachers that you loved and what they did well.

Meet weekly with co-teachers to discuss teaching strategies.

Create a blog or shared document with other teachers to collect creative teaching ideas.

Ask each other about the technology, software, or other tools that you are using.

Share your teaching notes with other teachers for them to contribute additional insights.

Conclusion

Because I believe strongly in learning from others, I invite you to contact me with strategies you've used to improve your own teaching or creative teaching ideas that you've found helpful. Finally, if this book has served you in a specific way, please let me know. I would enjoy the conversation. You can reach me at the following email address: teachingeutychus@ gmail.com.

REFERENCES

Allen, Holly Catterton, and Christine Lawton Ross. *Intergenerational Christian Formation: Bringing the Whole Church Together in Ministry, Community and Worship.* Downers Grove, IL: InterVarsity Press, 2012.

Ambrose, Susan A., Michael W. Bridges, Michele DiPietro, Marsha C. Lovett, and Marie K. Norman. *How Learning Works: 7 Research-based Principles for Smart Teaching.* San Francisco, CA: Jossey-Bass Publishers, 2010.

Anderson, L. W. & Krathwohl, D. R., eds. *A Taxonomy for Learning, Teaching, and Assessing: A Revision of Bloom's Taxonomy of Educational Objectives.* New York: Longman, 2001.

Brookfield, Stephen. *The Skillful Teacher: On Technique, Trust, and Responsiveness in the Classroom.* San Francisco: Jossey-Bass, Publishers, 2006.

Brueggemann, Walter. *Awed to Heaven, Rooted in Earth: Prayers of Walter Brueggemann.* Edited by Edwin Searcy. Minneapolis: Fortress Press, 2003.

————. *Prayers for a Privileged People.* Nashville: Abingdon Press, 2008.

Claibourne, Shane, Jonathan Wilson-Hartgrove, and Enuma Okoro. *Common Prayer: A Liturgy for Ordinary Radicals.* Grand Rapids, MI: Zondervan, 2010.

Counsell, Michael. *2,000 Years of Prayer.* Harrisburg, PA: Morehouse Publishers, 1999.

Laufenberg, Diana. Presentation entitled "How to Learn from Mistakes." New York: TED, 2010.

LeFever, Marlene. "Learning Styles." In *Introducing Christian Education*, Michael J. Anthony, ed. Grand Rapids, MI: Baker Academic, 2001.

Palmer, Parker J. *The Courage to Teach: Exploring the Inner Landscape of a Teacher's Life.* San Francisco: Jossey-Bass Publishers, 1997.

————. *Parker Palmer and the Courage to Teach.* 4 February. The Aurora Forum. Stanford University, 2009.

Pullias, Earl V., and James D. Young. *A Teacher Is Many Things.* Bloomington: Indiana University Press, 1968.

Tozer, A.W. *The Pursuit of God.* Harrisburg, PA: Christian Publications, 1948.

Wilhoit, James, David P. Setran, Donald Ratcliff, Daniel T. Haase, and Linda Rosema.

"Soul Projects: Class-Related Spiritual Practices in Higher Education." *Journal of Spiritual Formation and Soul Care* 2 (Fall 2009): 153-178.

Williams, Robin. *The Non-designers Design Book: Design and Typographic Principles for the Visual Novice*, 2nd ed. Berkeley, CA: Peachpit Press, 2004.

About the Author

Houston Heflin, EdD, is an assistant professor at Abilene Christian University in Abilene, Texas. He teaches in the undergraduate Bible department, the Graduate School of Theology, and the Honors College at ACU. He is a member of the North American Professors of Christian Education and the Society for the Study of Christian Spirituality. He serves as a volunteer teacher at his church and hosts teacher equipping seminars with churches across the United States. He authored, *Youth Pastor: The Theology and Practice of Youth Ministry* (2009). You can reach him at teachingeutychus@gmail.com.

CPSIA information can be obtained
at www.ICGtesting.com
Printed in the USA
FSOW01n0419280316
18420FS